Us Against Them

HOW TRIBALISM AFFECTS
THE WAY WE THINK

BY

BRUCE ROZENBLIT

Transcendent Publications
Kansas City, MO

Published by Transcendent Publications
P.O. Box 22547
Kansas City, MO 64113

Library of Congress Control Number 2008910226

ISBN 978-0-615-23316-1

Editorial Services by Marc D. Baldwin, PhD
www.edit911.com, Inc.

Cover Image by Eclecticollections

ACKNOWLEDGEMENTS

This book represents the thoughts and opinions of the author who is solely responsible for its content. The following individuals made a significant contribution to the book's development. The author wishes to express his deepest gratitude and appreciation for their input and guidance.

Dr. David Lawrence, Ph.D.
Associate Professor of Philosophy and Religion
University of North Dakota

Dr. Lawrence reviewed my core thesis which contained my major arguments. He provided lists of books for further study, and participated in numerous e-mail exchange discussing various subsequent arguments as they were developed.

Paul C. Jenkins, ABD
Anthropologist, United States Forest Service

Mr. Jenkins reviewed my core thesis and provided guidance regarding my understanding of basic principles of anthropology, prepared a list of books to study, and supplied several articles for my use.

Dr. Joseph Weeres, Ph.D.
Professor Emeritus
The Claremont Graduate University

Dr. Weeres reviewed my nearly completed manuscript and provided guidance that helped to greatly focus and sharpen the arguments presented.

Table of Contents

SCOPE AND INTENT

This is an investigation into the ways that tribalism affects human thought. This is not a scientific study where experiments were run, data was obtained, and conclusions drawn. Where possible, scientific evidence produced by other researchers is used in a corroborative fashion to support the arguments presented. This is a rationalist investigation using the philosophical method of induction/ deduction of how tribalism affected the evolution of the human mind. I have observed how people behave today and reverse-engineered how we might have gotten this way. I have developed an ordered series of developmental stages that provide a pathway, a methodology, from the past to the present by utilizing the principle that behavioral characteristics evolve just as physical characteristics evolve, and that process goes from elemental forms to more complicated ones. The simple elemental behavior always precedes the more complicated advanced behavior.

Observational data were obtained the old-fashioned way, by living life. I have thirty years of professional experience as a design engineer and business owner and interact with customers from all over the world. I have found that there is a tremendous similarity in the way people think and attempt to solve problems, suggesting that people from different cultures behave as one gigantic monolith. Why do so many people make the same types of mistakes when problem solving? Why is political propaganda so effective? There must be some common thread that runs through humanity that causes these behaviors, and I went looking for it. I attended the laboratory of life and utilized my own personal experiences and observations. This is exactly what the philosophers of old did. They did not have access to the technology of the modern world. All they had were their own experiences and observations and one other mighty tool: their thoughts. Archaic? Yes, but they were right about many things. Pure thought is a tremendously powerful problem-solver. Nowadays, we tend to push out with technology and then try to figure out what we have observed. A more traditional method is to push out with thought and then use technology to verify or disprove that thought.

Many scientists treat the unknown as a great jigsaw puzzle. They find a little piece and draw it in, then find another piece and draw it in, and then continue until a picture emerges. There is another way to explore the unknown.

If the principles of the formation and interaction of elements can be determined, then we can predict where these puzzle pieces are and how they will behave and interact, even if we can't observe them. Physics often utilizes this method of problem solving. The equations developed by physicists define the workings of the universe. Sometimes these equations are developed in response to observed data, but often times they are the result of pure thought. They are an attempt to predict phenomena that we cannot observe, such as what happens inside a black hole. Of course, observable data are required to verify the equations, but the lack of data does not invalidate the methodology used to produce its solutions. There are phenomena that we just don't have the ability to observe, but that doesn't stop people from trying to expand human knowledge and understand them.

This is how my mind works. I have a worldview similar to that of the physicist. Everything happens because of cause and effect relationships, and these relationships can be identified. They may be counterintuitive, such as with quantum mechanics, but they are rational in that they can be defined with equations or logical relationships. They may be comprised of random events, but the randomness is ordered and defined by other logical relationships. The actual outcomes of events are statistical in nature in that they are proportional to the cause. Causes lead to effects, but the effects are probabilistic.

This is not how a typical behavioral scientist looks at the world. They use a more empirically based method of testing and observing. What I have done is to violate this established methodology intentionally and use a methodology similar to a theoretical physicist. This will no doubt cause my findings to be rejected by many on purely procedural grounds, because that is just not the way "we" do these things. Obviously, I disagree.

I have read a stack of books about four feet high trying to educate myself on these matters of why we do what we do. I can tell you that for every position taken, there is a counter-position. Everyone is all over the map. Theories abound of all types with evidence that backs them up, and there are counter-theories with evidence that opposes them. There is no consensus.

How can everyone be right? Not possible. Maybe no one is right. It appears that what is accepted as right has more to do with the reputation of the theory-maker than anything else.

But I say science is about discovering the truth and not about reputations. The secrets of nature are contained in the principles that govern nature. Nature is revealed to us by understanding these principles.

The methodology used in the preparation of this book is one of applying rational thought to reveal unobservable phenomena: specifically, how did our minds evolve over the last 200,000 years to produce what we are today? So long as my reasoning is correct, then my solutions are plausible, provided the assumptions they are based on are plausible. "Plausible" means there is a scientific basis to support the assumptions. The accuracy of the solutions is then dependent on the assumptions being made.

All of the changes in the function of the human mind discussed here are influenced by natural selection. These changes are all based in improving the reproductive fitness of the human species, which has resulted in what we are to-day. This is the basis of the new field of evolutionary psychology. The architecture of my analysis is the same type of multi-linear thinking I use when designing and diagnosing electronic circuits. When an abnormality, or undesired response, is discovered in an electronic network, the cause of the abnormality is often not located at the site where it is observed. There could be many other places in the network that could contribute to, or cause, the abnormality. When examining these other places, additional abnormalities may be discovered that may or may not contribute to the original problem. Further complicating the situation is that, even if a secondary abnormality is found, there may be no observable direct cause/effect relationship to the primary abnormality, because the component where the secondary abnormality is found may test as functioning perfectly. The next step is then to search for other observable abnormalities and develop an overarching theory that connects all observable phenomena together and points to the offending culprit or culprits that are causing the problem that was initially observed. The theory may point to a component that may not even display any outward signs of malfunctioning. If the theory is correct, replacing the suspect component will "magically" clear up all primary and secondary abnormalities. As you can well imagine, this isn't easy, and can be very frustrating, to say the least. Virtually all electrical phenomena lie outside the realm of normal sensory perception and appear to our minds as abstractions.

Particularly difficult here is the use of mental abstractions to identify non-observable causes. In developing my theories and overarching arguments, I used this same problem solving technique and mental "tool kit" in the manner just described. I will use secondary observable phenomena that initially may appear to be merely anecdotal, but when combined with other corroborative phenomena and linked together with an overarching theory, the probability of identifying an ultimate cause is greatly increased. This linkage cannot prove causation, just as any theory of a faulty electronic component is not proven until the suspect component is replaced, but this methodology greatly increases the odds of doing so. Human behavioral science is highly subjective and controversial, and, as such, it may be impossible to prove any of my theories quantitatively. It may also be impossible quantitatively to disprove them.

Understanding why we do what we do requires tackling

sensitive issues and I will use politics as a primary explanatory mechanism, because politics dominates our culture. This is not an attempt to glorify or ridicule any group over any other. There will be people, probably more so on the political right than the political left, that may become angry with me for some of the things I will say. I want to emphasize that the arguments presented are not intended to prove inferior/superior behaviors, just what those behaviors are and why they happen. I will attempt to be respectful of people's religious convictions and will not try to prove or disprove whether such a thing as "religious truth" exists. Religion is an integral part of civilization, and any investigation of human behavior is incomplete without considering it. The arguments presented are focused on discovering the truth, and the conclusions reached will contradict what some religious beliefs dictate. In defense of the faithful, this does not mean religious truth does not exist. It does imply that a less literal interpretation of religious teachings is required to allow for the explanations of the world that science reveals to us. The term "tribal" will seem derogatory to some. It is not. "Tribal" terminology is a reflection of the human condition, just as is having a human body. The arguments presented are in no way an attempt to denigrate indigenous tribal societies or cast them as "primitive." All societies are tribal. This book is a process of discovery and not a process of condemnation.

In writing this book, I took a journey whose conclusions were not at all what I had expected. I let the arguments themselves flow to where ever the process and analysis led, rather in the manner of a 19th Century philosopher than a contemporary social scientist. This may force the reader to work a bit harder as they follow this journey with me, but our modern world could use a little more critical introspection instead of the constant bombardment of five-second sound bites. Learning isn't just about selling ideas; it's also about understanding ideas. Excellence in thought requires effort and practice, just as does athletic excellence.

As the following will show, tribalism shapes our thoughts, which ultimately shape our behavior, interacting with common, everyday mental operations and decision-making. Topics covered will include religious beliefs, political ideologies, scientific beliefs, economic ideologies, and just about every other "ology." The evidence may initially appear to be merely anecdotal, but when all is linked together with overarching arguments, it becomes much more significant, giving my theories more power and authority, just as with my example of diagnosing electronic circuits. What I hope ultimately to prove is that all of these categories of human culture are manifestations of the same global mental processes largely controlled by tribalism.

Innate Processes of the Mind

Tribalism is not just a component of human culture, but is also linked to the natural evolution of our biology. Understanding this requires understanding the links between behavior and biology. This opens up the ongoing and contentious debate concerning nature versus nurture. Academics line up on either side of this fault line, which is another effect of tribalism, as I will address later.

The human brain did not evolve independently from the rest of the animal kingdom. Actually, no organism or part of any organism evolved completely independently from the rest of the animal kingdom. Everything that is or ever was alive shares biological, physiological, and chemical processes and structures. We are all kin to each other.

Evolution manifests itself as a series of progressive events. The complexity of the creatures of the animal kingdom is the result of this progression starting with the first simple bacteria.

Evolution capitalizes on successful strategies, retains them, and adds additional features. There is a force in nature that causes these events to take place. Any change in an organism's form or function that allows it to increase its propagation and make more organisms will increase that characteristic in the organism's population. This force is called "natural selection." We say that such a characteristic "is selected" when this happens.

The essence of evolution is that all life forms are developing or "evolving" from a series of modifications from previous life forms passed on from generation to generation. These modifications may be almost imperceptible from one generation to the next, or they may be rapid, large changes. Either case does not invalidate evolution itself. The source of the modifications is random variations in an animal's genome. If any of these modifications give an animal a reproductive advantage over others, and this includes allowing the animal to thrive in a different environmental niche, the characteristics of these modifications will be amplified throughout the population, as these are the creatures that had the most offspring. We see this happening today when fish from a tropical region are injected into a North American river system and quickly crowd out everything else. The introduced species has both no natural predators and the characteristics to out-compete the native species for resources. In a very short time, the native species can be driven to extinction. This example shows how an adaptive advantage increases reproductive fitness. It does not show where the adaptive advantage came from, but it does show

how powerful it can be.

Natural selection is very simple, but this simple force can create an infinite variety of organisms. Currently, there are tens of millions of different types of creatures living on the earth. Over the history of the earth, that number is orders of magnitudes greater.

In addition to the physical structure of creatures, all creatures possess specific behavior. Even single-cell animals possess behavior. They respond to chemical stimuli and react accordingly. An example is the ion exchanges through cell membranes that regulate the animal's internal processes. The behavior in this case would be feeding by controlling how the animal absorbs nutrients from the environment (Clark and Grunstein, 2000). Single celled creatures need to eat just like we do.

Human behavior and culture are also the result of a progression of events from our early primal beginnings to modern civilization. This progression is just as much an evolutionary process as is our biology.

More complicated creatures have a specific organ, a brain that regulates their behavior. Brains do essentially two things: they regulate the internal physiological processes that sustain life, and they regulate an organism's outward behavior, which also is primarily concerned with sustaining life. A creature's behavior focuses on its ability to survive and reproduce. An organism that can't fly and consistently displays behavior such as jumping out of tall trees instead of climbing down will have trouble remaining alive long enough to reproduce. Behavior is just as significant a component of survival as sharp teeth and claws or a keen sense of smell used to find food. Natural selection operates on characteristics that affect survivability and procreation, so behavior is something that natural selection influences. We will concentrate on the outward behavior of humans, the choices we make and why we make them, and how natural selection may have altered and influenced how we make those choices through the mechanism of tribalism.

When I speak of biological influences on behavior is this book, I am speaking of these influences as tendencies that increase probabilities of outcomes. That does not mean that any particular individual will express these outcomes, just that an increased number of people in any given large population will. The net effect of these increased prob-abilities is that they can have a pronounced influence over population groups over time.

The question here is the degree of influence that biol-ogy has on these mental processes. Humans are not robots. We can learn, and learning has a huge effect on behavior. The arguments presented here are not just concerned with how biology affects the choices that minds make, but how biology affects how we learn and interpret reality, which greatly affects the choices our minds make. The cortex of the human brain is much larger and more complicated than any other animal (Goldberg, 2001). This feature gives our minds the ability to learn and reason unlike no other crea-ture, which has given rise to advanced cultures. Behavior is mostly learned and culturally transmitted between us. The net behavior that any individual displays is a combina-tion of cultural, or environmental, and heritable factors. How does this relationship express itself?

Do creatures share brain structures with other creatures? Yes, absolutely. Just as there are great similarities in the physiology and structure of animals, there is great similarity in the structures of brains. The same forces that shaped bodies and organs shaped brains. Reptiles have fish brain parts, and mammals have reptile and fish brain parts, and humans have other mammalian and reptile and fish brain parts (Carter, 1999). Natural selection retains things that work. This is why it operates so efficiently and can create such an incredible diversity of creatures. It's an additive process.

Do the brains of these earlier animals posses innate behaviors? Yes, they do. We often call this an animal's instinct. Can animals learn? Absolutely. The amount of learning depends on the sophistication of the animal's brain. Does the ability to learn completely nullify an animal's innate behaviors? No, it modifies them.

Creatures such as fish and reptiles hatch from eggs and have to take care of themselves very quickly. There is often little parental involvement. They have to be able to eat and avoid being eaten on their own. Nature must have preprogrammed their minds with the basic behaviors necessary for survival. Whether or not they can learn, they come into this world with a sufficient base of innate behaviors that give them the chance to survive and reproduce.

Mammals are a different case. Mammalian young are totally dependent on their mothers. Generally speaking, the more intelligent the mammal, the longer the offspring is attached to the mother. In primates, the bond can last for several years (De Waal, 2005). In humans, one would hope at least past age sixteen. The dependency is not totally caused by the lack of physical maturity of the offspring. It is also caused by the offspring's not knowing enough about how to survive on their own. They have to develop the skills necessary to forage, hunt, and avoid being hunted.

Mammals raised in captivity need their human caregivers to teach them how to forage and hunt. Even with their powerful physical assets, they still have to acquire skills to survive. Behavior is just as important to survival as physical function and form.

Learning cannot take place without something with which to learn. There has to be some minimum base of cognitive ability to enable any creature to learn. The animal then has a minimum innate cognitive base from which it can express a minimum base of innate behaviors. Does this mean that mammals and other higher life forms do not possess any innate behaviors? No, it does not. Nature has endowed them with basic instinctual behaviors. It does means that they require additional skills on top of these basic behaviors in order to survive. These skills are learned from the mother and/or father, practice, and social interaction and observation with others of their own kind. The innate behaviors are still there. Just because additional features of something are needed for improved function does not mean that any inherent features suddenly disappear.

Humans were formed from the same forces of nature and are susceptible to the same environmental pressures as other animals. We have very similar chemistry, physiology, form, structure, and needs as many other creatures. If the entire animal kingdom possesses innate behaviors, why would one single species out of millions not have it? From this perspective, it seems the burden of proof should lie with those that believe humans have no innate behaviors. Behavior is a component of biology, and humans share tremendous amounts of biology with all other creatures. Why, then, would humans be the only exception in the animal kingdom that does not have any innate behaviors? To make this assumption is to imply that humans are something other than members of the animal kingdom, and the legacy of our biology and physiological function completely contradicts that assumption.

Let's look at some specific evidence that demonstrates that humans actually do have innate behavioral characteristics.

The Minnesota Twins study (Pinker, 2002) investigated the behavioral habits and characteristics of identical twins separated at birth and raised in different environments. The study subjects had a great deal of common behavioral characteristics, such as both twins' preferring green cotton shirts and preferring the same singer. The results of the study suggest that about 50% of the variability of human behavior results from genetic factors. That means about 50% of the things that I do that you don't result from biological sources. The figure of 50% does not apply to any particular behavior, but is a net average of all possible behaviors combined. The study shows that a large identifiable percentage of behavioral differences are genetic, regardless of what the genetic component of any particular behavior is. What about the general case of the whole of humanity? Do humans possess species-wide behaviors? The field of evolutionary psychology investigates the evolutionary aspects of various types of social behaviors, including sexual selection, parenting, altruism, reciprocal altruism, pairing, kin relationships, and many other aspects of human behavior (Pinker, 2002; Ridley, 1996, 2003; Barrett, 2002).

There are mechanisms in the genome that can help to explain the interaction between environment and biology.

It has been determined that there are about three billion strands of human DNA but only about 30,000 genes actually code for the proteins that make up a human being. That is not much information, considering the immense complexity of a human. We are just beginning to unravel the secrets of life. Much of DNA is promoter DNA, which serves as a regulatory mechanism for the coding of proteins (Richards and Hawley, 2005). Promoter DNA acts like a set of thermostats that turns genes on and off. But what is it regulating in response to? If it acts like a thermostat, then it controls a variable parameter against a desired set point. Therefore, promoter DNA has to be able to monitor some parameter according to which it is controlling genetic activity. For example, a thermostat monitors the temperature in a building and then activates the furnace or the air conditioner. When the desired temperature is reached, the furnace or AC shuts off. Because promoter DNA functions as a regulatory mechanism, it must interact with the metabolic environment and that environment is influenced by behavior. The environment influences what genes do, so the two cannot be separated. The behavior of an organism functions in the same way. What people do depends on the interaction between culture and biology.

There is another way that genes interact with the environment. There are chemicals in the body that can attach themselves to strands of DNA and activate or deactivate genes. This new field of study is called epigenetics. Any environmental influences that cause metabolic processes to increase or decrease the amount of these chemicals will have a direct effect on genetic activity, the making of proteins. This biological feature provides a direct chemical link to genetic activity, which potentially can affect the structure and behavior of humans. A fascinating field indeed.

Another reason for the large number of strands of DNA

is that there are dormant sections left over from our evolutionary past. It may ultimately be possible to unravel secrets of our evolutionary development by decoding and understanding these dormant strands. We are indeed just beginning to understand what makes us tick.

There is great ongoing debate about the significance and dominance in the behavioral sciences about these interactions. A personal experience illustrates my position.

I have always tested well in abstract reasoning, math, and logic skills. My verbal skills have always tested in the average range (maybe high average on a good day). Schematics, mechanical diagrams and concepts, mental visualization of complicated assemblies, calculations, deductive reasoning: this type of thinking has always been easy for me. I have always had a difficult time with words. Thoughts flow through my mind, and I often have trouble generating the words to translate them adequately into sentences. I would rather draw a diagram or write an equation. I have met many people where words flow like a waterfall. I think to myself, how do they generate so many words so easily? I'm not like that. Why?

I was born that way. I have natural abilities to engage in some mental processes more than others. This is no different from athletic talent, musical talent, or any other kind of talent. We are all like this and all have talents and weaknesses (Gardner, 2004). I want to emphasize that environment, or cultural influences, have just as much to do with being good at something as does natural talent. Yes, it takes talent to play in the NBA or sing at the Metropolitan Opera, but it also requires tens of thousand of hours of practice and training. A person with no talent who undergoes the same training doesn't achieve the same level of performance as the gifted person does, though they can certainly improve. My writing ability has improved dramatically over the years (actually more like decades), but I will never write a decent novel or good poetry. I will say that every time I attempt a writing project, it gets just a little bit easier. A problem with formal education is that when a person is in school, they don't have a decade or two improve; they only have a few months. So everyone does the same thing. They avoid all the types of classes that they know they will have trouble with when these are precisely the classes they should be taking. I only had to take three hours of English in college. I needed thirty. Likewise, English majors would benefit from a couple dozen hours of algebra, geometry, statistics, and logic. The Second Coming will occur before that happens. High performance requires talent and training and time, lots of time.

Cultural or environmental influences pushed me into engineering. I could have just as easily become a physicist, an accountant, a statistician, or pursued some other analytical career if the necessary cultural influences were provided to me. Biologically implanted characteristics do not mandate outcomes; they mandate tendencies. They mandate sensitivities to environmental stimuli. We are not predetermined by our genes for any specific type of behavior (excluding genetically induced disease). We are predetermined to be more sensitive to and respond more vigorously to certain environmental stimulations. Our biology then establishes probabilities that certain outcomes will materialize. Because of my natural talents, the probability of my ending up in a field such as engineering was much higher than the probability of my becoming a journalist.

Societal Organization

Human evolution has not ceased, but there is a point in our development where humans are generally regarded as becoming "modern." If these behaviors originated before our brains reached their modern form, then direct comparisons between contemporary hunter-gatherer societies and ancient humans are not completely valid, because ancient humans did not have the mental machinery that we do. I hate to use the term "primitive" when describing contemporary hunter-gatherers, because these people are fully modern humans with the same set of mental hardware that all humans have. It is chauvinistic to categorize modern humans from pre-industrialized societies as being cognitively something less than the rest of us. Studying their behavior gets us a little closer to understanding the fundamentals of human social organization, but it doesn't get us to the beginning.

As discussed above, modern human behavior is a result of a progression of events and development. This does not mean that societal outcomes are certain or universal, but it does provide an explanation for why history keeps repeating itself.

"Tribe" refers to a type of human societal organization which numbers at least a thousand individuals organized in communities of several hundred. Central control is firmly established with a chiefdom (Johnson and Earle, 2000). The behaviors that I assign to tribalism actually are a set of group-inspired behaviors that humans use to distinguish the in-group and the out-group, the "us" and "them." These behaviors had their roots in human society long before tribes actually existed and became more fully entrenched as formal tribes developed. They remain a major component of contemporary society.

The basic unit of human social organization is generally regarded as the family. The next level of societal complexity would be an assemblage of several families, or "bands," which would usually number from twenty-five to fifty individuals. The most basic type of band incorporates a hunter-gatherer organization. These groups are essentially egalitarian with no private property or organizational hierarchy. There would be no offices to hold, no political power. Some individuals could attain higher status in the group, but no one would be officially in charge. Behavioral codes would be enforced by interpersonal relationships (Johnson and Earle, 2000).

By observing the behavior of contemporary hunter-gatherer societies, we can speculate that their behavior is an indication of some of the practices of ancient humans. Assuming that these modern behaviors result from reacting to environmental pressures that have existed for many tens of thousands of years, it is reasonable to assume that ancient humans responded in a similar, although less complicated fashion. Similarly, there is some validity in comparing the behavior of chimpanzees to ancient humans when our minds were less developed. Since humans and chimpanzees share a great deal of physiology and morphology, it is reasonable to assume that each species would adopt similar behaviors in response to the same environmental pressures, so long as these behaviors lie within the physical and mental capabilities of each species. Realizing that both species evolved along separate paths, common behaviors cannot be viewed as absolutely conclusive regarding their origins, but they do serve as useful indicators (De Waal, 2005). This argument could be extended to the entire animal kingdom, but it is most relevant when made comparing chimpanzees to humans, because we are so closely related.

This does not mean that early human organizational structures were egalitarian. Animal groups usually have a dominant individual. The earliest human group structures very possibly employed such a leader. Egalitarianism may be a cultural advance that modern humans developed as an efficient way to structure hunter-gather societies. But history shows us that central control was to become the dominant format for human society as organizational structures became more complicated. Until the advent of the modern secular democratic state, dictatorships, monarchies, and totalitarian regimes ran the world.

What would cause ancient people to band together in the first place? Why not just remain independent families? The field of ecology investigates these questions. For any creature to survive and reproduce, it must expend energy to secure the resources it needs to thrive. The difficulty here is that these resources are often not widely available, and many other creatures also want to consume them. Survival in the wild is a matter of besting the competition in the acquisition of the things needed to stay alive. Hardly a trivial manner.

The less energy a creature has to expend to secure these resources, the better the chances of survival. Animals with plenty to eat tend to be strong and fit, allowing them to escape predation and secure mates. The weak ones usually end up as another's dinner. Creatures that possess higher levels of intelligence, such as wolves, whales, apes, and people, can incorporate social cooperation to acquire resources and defend themselves more efficiently. Social cooperation then has a direct bearing on the efficiency of resource acquisition.

Lions have prides, wolves have packs, and baboons have bands, and so do people. These groupings are all employed to enhance survivability. Human beings have had to adapt to the same environmental pressures as many other creatures and, as a result, have incorporated group behavior as a solution to these problems.

Social interaction between groups involves the opposing strategies of conflict versus cooperation. How much of each depends on population density, availability of resources, and level of complexity of social organization. With very low population densities of no more than one person per square mile, modern humans tend to organize themselves in small family bands that cooperate with each other and try to avoid conflict by moving into different areas to forage. So long as there is plenty of room for these small groups to avoid each other, conflict is held to a minimum. This has the effect of limiting population growth, because it only works with population densities of less than one person per square mile. What are the factors that have caused population densities to swell to tens of thousands per square mile in modern cities? Population growth is fostered by the way people organize themselves into groups by societal structure and/or through technology. Anthropologists call this process "intensification" (Johnson and Earle, 2000). Through intensification, humans are able to increase population densities and group size continuously all the way to the nation state and even empire. There are many categories of group organization that have been assigned on an economic basis involving the acquisition and distribution of resources. This is the political economy in action.

In band-level human societies, social cooperation is based on interpersonal relationships. Since there is no formal structure that organizes these societies, my theories regarding belief based organization would not yet apply. At some unknown point or points, a minimal level of social complexity evolved where belief systems were used to organize society. This does not mean that these early people did not have beliefs. The only restriction to not having beliefs is not having the cognitive ability to generate them. Belief systems were not used at this time to organize society and delineate groups, because there wasn't enough societal complexity to require such delineation. Observational evidence exists that establishes this level as the "local group," which are groupings of up to around five hundred individuals organized under a leader. This level of organization dates back at least 10,000 years. Using the local group as a starting point does not mean that belief systems were not used as social organizing systems before the emergence of the local group. Human burial rituals have been found that date back for several tens of thousands of years indicating beliefs used as a component of culture. The next level of societal complexity is the "tribe," which is a grouping of at least one thousand individuals organized in several or more local groups with firm control in the hands of a chiefdom. By this level of complexity, the chief may not have been selected, but may have taken power. Language would have been fully implemented by now, which is crucial for the transmission and implementation of belief systems as a component of culture and social organization (Johnson and Earle, 2000).

Conflict between groups had become an integral part of tribal life and human social development. Many studies tend to paint a picture of the distant past as being very peaceful with little group conflict. Yet having foragers living in family level groups that utilized avoidance to minimize conflict doesn't mean they were not capable of conflict. It means they tried to avoid it, and low population densities and ample resources allowed for that avoidance. By the time our ancestors reached the local group structure, combat was an integral part of life. Population densities had reached the point where people had to take what they needed and keep others from the same scarce resources. It is apparent from human history that the larger and more complicated societies become, the greater, more frequent, and more intense the conflict. Indeed, the tendency for group violence is inside all of us, and it emerges when environmental pressures call it forth (Smith, 2007). Group violence is a component of our distant animal past. Have you ever witnessed a riot? Mild-mannered people do terrible things to others. These behaviors are not rational; they are emotional, indicating that their roots lay deep in our past when we didn't have the capacity for rational moderation of behavior. Even now, when we have the cognitive capacity, we still can't control them; we still riot. That shows us how deeply ingrained and powerful these behaviors are. Group violence must be an innate component of us all.

The issue of survivability not only involves finding food. It involves avoiding predation and murder by members of the same species. Quite simply, there is safety in numbers. Anyone that has ever lived in a rough neighborhood or attended rough schools quickly learns that concept. Animals, particularly predatory animals, often establish territories and fiercely drive out or kill members of their own species for trespassing. Groups compete against each other for scarce natural resources. We were and are a brutal species. In contemporary hunter-gatherer societies, an average of about 30% of males die in combat. Typically, small raiding parties of three or more males would search the countryside near their territorial perimeters for lone males of another tribe. If they found one, he would be chased down and killed. This type of behavior is duplicated in chimpanzee societies, where about 30% of male chimps also die from such combat. I don't think the chimps are imitating us. They were here before we were. This is not to say that our raiding behavior is derived from the chimpanzee, but it might indicate that humans have responded to the same environmental pressures as chimpanzees in the same way and consequently developed similar raiding behaviors (Smith, 2007; Wade, 2006; Sanderson, 2001).

A male human no longer in the group has a decreased chance for survival. It certainly reduces chances of reproduction. The odds of being killed by another group or by predators would be greatly increased without the protection of the group. Any behavioral characteristics that contributed to group rejection would tend to be weeded out. This would tend to select for the characteristics desired by the group in the population.

Females were probably treated differently. In hunter-gatherer societies, raids were conducted to steal females for breeding purposes. If females were often stolen for breeding, then the possibility of a rejected female's being accepted by another group is real. In chimpanzee society, females migrate to other tribes to prohibit inbreeding, which forms a precedent in primates for the movement of females between groups.

Instead of massive organized battles, war was typically implemented by conducting raids against competing groups, and over time losses could be huge. Groups could even be raided to extinction (Smith, 2007). These raids were not necessarily conducted as a response to another raid. They were often preemptive strikes, in which groups would "attack to defend." As rival groups increase in strength, they become greater threats to security, so the thinking goes, so let's attack them before they attack us. (Where have I heard this before?) This behavioral characteristic indicates that the group, or more recently the tribe, has long been firmly established as a means of identifying whom to kill and whom to support. We did it then, and we do it now.

Combat between groups is directly related to the availability of resources and population density (Johnson and Earle, 2000). The more people per square mile, the lesser the amount of food per person, and the greater the chances of conflict. If food abounds, why spend the energy to fight off a rival group? It's much easier to ignore them and forage. I would venture to guess that during the course of human history, this scenario was probably rare and intermittent at best. Nature doesn't provide a Garden of Eden for very long. The good stuff goes fast. As resources become scarce and/or populations expand, groups become more territorial. This is when the fighting breaks out, the beginning of the "us" against the "them." This is not to say that groups did not trade and cooperate with each other. They did. The impetus to my argument is demonstrating the importance of group organization to human culture and thought, with trade's being a part of that mix. However, people don't trade away things that they need. Trading activity implies that surplus materials exist for that trade. When resources become scarce and survival is at stake, people take what they need from wherever they can take it.

This may be an obvious point, but it needs to be stated. As human organizational systems evolved and grew into large, formal communities and ultimately nation states, combat between groups certainly did not abate. History shows us that it just kept getting worse. As communities became more complex, combat strategies became more complex and lethal. The lethal nature of war has continued on an upward spiral from initial raiding behavior to world war. People just keep getting better at killing each other. This is an effect of tribalism on modern society.

The group solution is a common and ancient solution to the fiercely competitive nature of life in the wild, employed by countless numbers of species, as well as by humans. There is every reason to believe that our ancestors lived in groups at very early stages of our development, possibly dating back millions of years. Group associations are literally part of our DNA.

Intelligence is required for social interactions. Many scientists believe that the requirement for social behavior was the driving force that natural selection used to install the high intelligence that humans have evolved to possess. This would strongly indicate that social behavior greatly improves reproductive fitness.

The counter-argument is that intelligence itself greatly increases reproductive fitness by creating better ways of doing things through the means improved technology, and that social behavior is a beneficial side-effect of the intelligence. My disagreement with this position is that ancient humans could cooperate with each other before the advent of technology. The use of technology is not a prerequisite for social cooperation as is demonstrated by many animal species. By not requiring technology, the odds are increased that socialization drove the formation of high intelligence, which allowed for the development of technology.

Human infants experience tremendous cognitive growth during the first year of life, and this growth is the result of the stimulation of emotional and social interaction between the caregivers and the child. The child actually develops the ability to think logically as a result of these emotional and social interactions (Greenspan and Shanker, 2004).

This means the child doesn't initially develop the ability to perform tasks by doing tasks, but develops the cognitive ability to perform tasks from the stimulation provided by social and emotional interaction. This provides an indication of how our minds are likely to have developed in the past, as fetal and infant development is a window into our evolutionary past. Fetal brain development is not completed at birth. The cranial capacity of the baby greatly increases during the first year of life, because the size of brain we need to function fully as humans is much larger than can fit through the mother's birth canal. As a result, natural selection retards the development of the baby's brain in the fetal stage to reduce its size and the deficit is made up mostly during the first year. The emotional interactions experienced during the early years are absolutely crucial to the formation of the child's cognitive abilities. Children that are denied the necessary emotional and social stimulation as infants don't just suffer from emotional problems when they grow up, they also can have cognitive deficiencies, which can be severe, depending on the level of neglect. That's a fancy way of saying that they won't grow up to be as smart as they could have been. If the foundation of intelligence in modern humans is emotional and social interaction, then that foundation must have an origin. Our current condition is a strong indication that the origins of our intelligence developed along this very same path. Intelligence and social behavior are inexorably linked.

Larger groups can swallow up or kill off smaller competitors. They can more efficiently utilize technology and labor specialization to extract resources that further increase populations. Since the beginning of civilization, as groups expand, they don't often appear to fragment and splinter into new groups. Existing groups just keep getting bigger. Colonization is a part of that expansion. All through recorded history, nations and empires have constantly engaged in conquest in an attempt to grow. Continuous conquest is the saga of the history of civilization in the east, the west, the old, and the new world.

As human social organization advanced and social cooperation was enacted between non-relatives, a means of bonding individuals into cohesive groups was required. Initially, shared activities would have formed these bonds. The more significant the activity, the stronger the bonding effect. People's most essential activities are related to survival and reproduction.

Since the whole purpose of group structure is to enhance survival, the types of activities with which the political economy would be primarily engaged would also be the same. Finding enough food to eat, having shelter from the elements, securing mates, and acquiring protection from predators and other humans would dominate. These concerns are quite different from the motivations of a modern industrialized consumer society where productivity is maximized through market capitalism. These are two different conditions. Ancient hunter-gatherer life was not centered on the production of goods. The technology was not yet available to create a consumer society. Yes, people made tools and artifacts and articles of clothing and traded them with other groups, but the primary expenditure of energy was engaging in activities that directly kept the group alive.

The greater the intensity of the struggle, the greater the

bonding effect between group members. Talk to a combat veteran, and they will often tell you that the greatest sense of brotherhood and camaraderie they have ever experienced was with their fellow soldiers during battle. I ask the reader to reflect on their own life. When did you feel most connected to others? Was it during an intense struggle, such as a difficult project at work or during a team sporting event? Did this feeling of connectedness occur from everyone pursuing their self-interest or from sacrifice and expending energy for the good of the group?

As our minds progressed, a profound new component to group activity arose. Since people engaged in group behavior to accomplish tasks that enhanced survivability, as soon as the concept of belief became established, people could engage in activities that they *believed* would enhance survival. It wasn't just the doing of things together to stay alive; it was also *believing in the doing of things together* that became important. The actual activity may or may not have anything to do with survivability, but if it were believed that it did, the activity would become just as emotionally significant as *if* it did. I am speaking of the interjection of myth, superstition, and belief into human culture and the political economy.

A means of communicating these beliefs would have been required, or else they never could have become a component of group culture. This could have occurred before the emergence of language through the use of movement as a communicative medium. Rudimentary rituals, for example, could have provided such a function in humans. In today's world, shaking hands or bowing would be examples of such defined behavior. Ritual behavior has to be consistently defined within the group. Cultural systems of such definition were then frameworks for behaviors and the beliefs they represented. These frameworks of shared behaviors would be an important step in establishing a means of tribal identification that utilized higher order thinking. This would be a major component in defining the "us." *The group is now defined not by just what they do together, but also by their shared beliefs.*

Long before we had powerful minds that created myths and religions, we lived in groups, as do many animal species, such as wolves, baboons, dolphins, and others. The development of group organization is the result of evolution. Certain species evolved to incorporate group-based societies, while others live almost completely solitary lives. The original need for humans to live in groups has its origins in biology, not advanced human culture. It is culture, specifically belief systems as a group-binding device, which has improved what biology installed in us before our minds developed into the powerhouses they now are. My reasoning is that natural selection operates on any feature that increases an animal's reproductive fitness. Our ability to create culture was a new feature that could be modified by natural selection just as soon as the feature began to materialize. In other words, just as natural selection has crafted the amazing wing of the hawk from the origins of the simple membrane wing of flying dinosaurs, it shaped our conscious minds to bind us into groups as our intellects developed.

What cultural systems shaped the first social binding frameworks of behavior? What purpose did they serve? Survival was a full-time job and would have been the primary focus of human activity. The essential elements of survival and reproduction are food, water, shelter from the elements, combat, and the pairing of males and females. The first frameworks would most likely be concerned with the acquisition and distribution of these essential elements, such as a fertility dance or a type of body paint intended to insure a good hunt. But what cultural system would have been most likely used to shape these frameworks of behavior? Religion was the initial cultural system used as a framework of this more advanced social behavior.

Religion and Belief Systems

Belief systems are frameworks of explanations that define some purpose or activity that satisfies desires.

These early belief systems would have defined activities or the purpose of activities to satisfy the desire to survive. The activity could have been a ritual, such as drawing a symbol on the ground with a stick before the hunt. All that was necessary was, hypothetically speaking, that drawing the symbol was believed to enhance the hunt. Modern-day superstitions work in the same manner. Break a mirror and bad things will happen to you. Once our ancestors became smart enough to ask questions such as, "Why are we here?" and "Where did the world come from?" would complicated mythology be required to answer these questions. This assumes that the concept of staying alive preceded the question of "Why are we here?" Complicated mythology relates to providing explanations of reality, primarily explanations of existence and being, which is more sophisticated than a simple superstitious ritual like smearing berry juice on your forehead when seeking a mate. Simple behaviors would seem to precede more complicated behaviors.

Ancient proto-religions were then most likely expressed as an assortment of these ritual behaviors initially intended to communicate the desire to survive. Inclusion of the deity would have occurred later as cultural systems became more sophisticated, and is not a prerequisite for the invention of the ritual. Such rituals are then behaviors that bind people into groups through shared activities performed with the intent to communicate a desire to increase the survivability of the group. The binding effect is provided by the emotional significance of the ritual, which is very high because the ritual is associated with enhancing survival.

A ritual is then a common activity defined by a common belief system in order to satisfy a common desire. This is the essence of social binding.

Belief systems, primarily religion, define the rituals that bind us into groups through the enactment of communal activities primarily intended to enhance survival.

Let's list a possible sequence of events of these processes to explain further how all this could have unfolded. Of course this is speculative, as conclusive evidence does not exist.

1. People need to stay alive.

2. People formed small groups, initially with relatives, to share labor and resources. This increased reproductive fitness.

3. As the mind advanced and more complicated social behavior became possible, people banded together in larger groups that were not biologically related to each other. The members of the larger group shared labor and resources, which increased reproductive fitness even more. This is the advent of social cooperation and reciprocal altruism.

4. Groups competed against each other for scarce natural resources. Competition involved killing members of other groups or even eliminating entire groups.

5. Because group structure identifies targets for killing and support, a means is necessary to define who is in the group and who is not. The more advanced mind now develops cultural systems to define group membership.

6. These cultural systems are manifested in communally shared ritual behavior. These behaviors are intended to increase survivability by assuring a good hunt, good weather, fertility, success in combat, and similar desired outcomes. The behavior displayed is defined by the cultural system and is understood throughout the group to mean the same thing. This allowed the shared behavior to function as an efficient communicative mechanism.

7. Shared behavior that possesses universally accepted meaning forms the beginning of a means of identifying group membership. Performing the same tasks together to achieve a common desired outcome is a social binding mechanism, because the desired outcome can only be attained as the product of a group effort. Any cultural device that improves the cohesiveness of the group will have a positive impact on the group's survival.

8. Higher order thinking allows that the desired outcome be predicated by a belief. The practice of a ritual is now driven by a belief. It is now possible for a communally shared belief to function as a social binding mechanism because the source of the ritual is a belief.

9. Because these rituals are believed to enhance survival, they attain the highest emotional significance to the individual. They are things people do to stay alive. This causes the mind to associate performing rituals with staying alive. Therefore, not participating in rituals is rejecting what the group believes is activity required to stay alive, which forms a basis, or motivation, for rejecting the non-participant.

10. The belief system is then directly associated with survival, and following the belief system is viewed as supporting the group's survival. To reject the belief system is to threaten the survivability of the group, which is ample motivation for expulsion or even extermination. Belief systems then provide a means to define who is in the group and who is not by identifying whom to support and whom to kill. The belief system then defines group membership.

11. Belief systems evolved into formal religion by including mythology and deity worship to provide explanations of existence and being. Religion defines the tribe.

What observational evidence do I have to support these conclusions? The evidence is human history. First is the issue of targeting the "out" group, the "them." The following is not an inherent characteristic of religion, but results from the use of religion as an instrument of group identification.

All through recorded history, there has probably been no more frequently used justification for killing people than religion (Harris, 2004). People have been willing slaughter each other in the name of religion for millennia. Not only that, people have been willing to march onto the battle-field and sacrifice their own lives for religion. We react so strongly to religion that it can even break the blood bond between close family members. Children who reject their parents' religion could be ostracized from the family. Fathers commit "honor" killings and murder their daughters for being victims of sexual assault. Only ideas that convey the highest emotional significance can motivate such extreme behavior. The degree of emotional significance determines the level of motivation for carrying out the action. Why do we kill entire groups of people? Because they belong to different tribes. Why do we kill and die for religion? Because religion defines the tribe. This is the action of tribalism. We kill each other because of tribalism, not because of religion.

What positive effects have I observed religion to foster?

Religion gives people a sense community, a sense of belonging. How many times have you heard religious people describe fellow believers with phrases such as, "religious community" or "our community of faith" or just "our community"? Why does the word "community" keep popping up? Because that is exactly what it is, a community. It's the "us." This is not a geographic "us," or a national "us," or an ethnic "us," but a belief-based "us." Have you ever heard religious people refer to other members of their faith as "brother" or "sister"? This implies a familial connection fostered by the common belief that is a very strong "us." Nuns are called "sisters," monks are called "brothers." This again is the familial tie. "Come into the fold" is another phrase implying a grouping of people by belief. The purpose of these phrases is to identify groups, and those groups are defined by beliefs.

Religion gives people a sense of purpose. The world can be a very scary and dangerous place. Very bad things can happen to very good, very innocent people. Life presents itself to us as a mystery. Why are we here? What are we supposed to do while we are here? What happens to us when we are gone? There are droughts, floods, epidemics, and all sorts of calamities that cause great anxiety, so we try to make sense of it all. Religion helps us do that. It provides answers to these questions or, at least, functions as a soothing emollient to relieve our suffering. People do suffer in this world, often quite a lot. There is a never-ending need for things that help us feel better. I think it is a safe prediction that the world will never become an idyllic utopia where no one suffers.

Religion provides for codes of conduct. The rules and regulations of everyday life, dictated by many religions, provide us with a playbook of how to live our lives. Many people find this kind of structure very appealing. Civilization requires structure and order or civilization can't exist. Individuals also require structure to regulate and integrate their daily lives. Regular and repeatable events, such as religious rituals and worship activities, provide this type of structure. People need to share activities in order to feel grounded in a community, or we start to feel a little lost, adrift, disconnected from the group. I have met many people that need this kind of structure so intensely that they actually create their own schedules and routines and stick to them as if the world would come to a halt if they deviated. The schedule gives them a sense of purpose and importance. It's as if the person is saying, "I have to do this now because the activity is important, and that makes me feel important!" Orthodox religious traditions provide extreme rigor in how they structure daily life, which imparts a sense of purpose and importance to the individual.

I would venture to guess that it is this rigor that attracts people to pursue these endeavors as much as it is the desire for spiritual fulfillment.

The types of codes of conduct that religion provides are usually centered on what we call "morality." But religion does not create morality if morality is a product of the evolution of social cooperation (Hauser, 2006; Tancredi, 2005). Morality is an essential component of living together, a way that people interact with each other. How can a person live an immoral life in solitude? Immoral behavior requires another person to judge it immoral. The whole business of morality involves social interaction, such as "thou shalt" and "thou shalt not." A primary function of religion is to codify and tabulate moral codes, and this functioned as an early government as civilization advanced. There are plenty of religious codes that we find reprehensible today, such as human sacrifice and stoning people to death, which indicates that a behavioral code required by any religion is not a guarantee to achieve any absolute threshold of "good." I am not going to attempt to define what "good" is and will leave that up to the philosophers. However, the people that practiced these behaviors found them to be essential requirements of a properly run life regardless of how they appear to a 21st Century American. The issue is not one of pursuing an ultimate ethos, but one of tribal identity. We participate in these activities because they define the requirements of tribal membership.

Religion powerfully binds people into groups through the observance of holidays and ritual celebrations. Ritual celebrations punctuate and enrich our lives, and we tend to organize our lives around these events. They help us mark the passage of time with their regular occurrences and give us something to look forward to. Most important of all, they are things we do together as they are community-based activities. Some celebrations involve coming together in large groups, usually in a house of worship. This creates a strong fellowship. Families may celebrate holidays independently from each other, but these celebrations all happen at the same time, and people often enjoy sharing experiences of their independent celebrations with others. Rituals include rites of passage from childhood to adulthood, marriage, the end of life, and other important milestones. All of these activities are social binding mechanisms, because they pull us into cohesive units. Their primary importance is not rooted in pleasing a deity or the avoidance of punishment by a deity, but the coming together, the doing of something that lots of other people are doing. Many religious rituals are performed on a periodic basis and are intended to foretell some supernatural or cosmic event. Each time the ritual is performed, the supernatural event never occurs, without fail. Any reasonable person would say, "Why bother?" But reasonable people perform these rituals year-in and year-out and often look forward to the opportunity. Why? The outcome that never comes is not why we keep performing the rituals. This isn't about logic. It's performing the ritual that satisfies basic emotional needs, the need to be bound into groups. They make us feel as though we are not alone, like we are all part of something greater, even if almost everyone in the group doesn't believe that the desired outcome will materialize. The common activity inspired by a common belief defines the tribe. This is a major function of the holiday celebration. Perhaps all of the flack recently about the words "Happy Holidays" versus "Merry Christmas" has more to do with tribal identity than religious observance.

A Theory of the Origin of Religion

In order to maintain mental stability, the human mind must be able to differentiate between fantasy and reality. In order to establish mental concepts of reality, our minds must be able to define reality. The inability to do this is a type of clinically defined insanity. It is essential for proper mental function and stability that the mind generates these definitions.

The absence of definitions, or explanations of reality, creates anxiety, and our minds don't like that, causing us to adopt or invent explanations to relieve this anxiety. Are you really reading, this or do you just think you are reading this? Is your existence a dream? Are you really there, or are you the result of a hallucination? Whose hallucination? Yours or someone else's?

A person considering these questions valid might go into a panic. I certainly would get very worried if I seriously doubted that I am really here. This type of reaction to uncertainty of the self is a prime motivation for the generation of explanations of reality. Religion has long been utilized as a means of providing these explanations. As a basic human need, our minds require solutions to these perceived problems and mysteries of existence. We must relieve anxiety by understanding the unknown. This need is so great that people have probably been generating solutions to the question of existence since we first had the mental capacity to do so. The philosopher Daniel Dennett writes in *Breaking the Spell* of "the belief in belief" (Dennett, 2006). We have to have beliefs, because we have to have explanations of the unknown, principally the reasons for existence and being.

What types of belief does any particular mind generate or accept? This must be heavily influenced by the emotional needs of the individual, which ultimately are set by a combination of genetic and cultural factors. But people have common emotional needs, and people experience common cultural influences. Through the mechanism of culture, large numbers of people will accept common beliefs that satisfy their common emotional needs.

My arguments indicate that religion, or more generally belief systems that provide emotionally satisfying explanations of mysterious phenomena, satisfy a fundamental human need. The purpose of these explanations is to alleviate the anxiety caused by these very mysteries. Belief systems are then a fundamental component of human society. The common emotional needs of people allowed these explanations to be adopted and followed by large groups through the mechanism of cultural transmission. This is how religion became such a dominant factor in tribal identification.

Religion is then a necessary component of human culture. By connecting the two problems of tribal identification and the relief of mental anxiety with the same solution of religion, my arguments are made even stronger that the need for belief systems in human society has an innate component to it. One could argue that this innate tendency was placed in humans by a supernatural power and is a justification for the existence of religious truth. A good philosopher should consider all possibilities. I will leave that argument up to the reader. The need for religion may very well be solely produced by our biology. Another possibility is that biology has nothing to do with any of these features and they are purely the result of the evolution of human culture. I am inclined not to accept the culture-only solution because of the ferocity, intensity, and universality of these behaviors that have transcended cultural and geographic barriers throughout recorded history.

This is why the debate over whether religion should or should not be a component of public life is so hotly contested. It may be a biological issue, as religion may very well be a part of what we are as a species. Throughout history until the emergence of the United States, state religion was a constant feature of human society. An occurrence that keeps happening is no coincidence. The emergence of the United States as a secular liberal democracy may actually be in conflict with our biology. That is not to infer that a secular liberal democracy is inferior. With a pluralistic society, a secular liberal democracy is the best solution people have developed so far to allow different religions to coexist under the same government. Perhaps our society is having growing pains as we try to move past what our biology, our tribalism, dictates.

Can we get along without religion? Most people don't want to peer into the very essence of existence and ponder issues such as ultimate realities and the nature of truth. They just want to feel secure and happy. They seek tranquility and comfort. People have a right to seek out any beliefs that satisfy their needs. These needs are not delineated by intellect, or rationalization, or sophistication. They are delineated by emotional requirements. None of us ever asked to be born, but we are all here. The world truly is a scary and dangerous place. If religion makes the journey of life easier and more comfortable for people, then we should allow it.

Using a broader perspective, beliefs are more than something people do. It can be argued that beliefs are what people are. Human culture creates society. But what creates human culture? Belief systems do. All of the rules of conduct, values, morality, priorities and the like that create any human society are defined by beliefs. It is our beliefs that define what we are as a people no matter who "we" are. It is not important that any of these beliefs be provable or logical, because human beings are not primarily logical and rational. We are primarily emotional, and the satisfaction of our emotional needs is what drives us. Our minds do not tolerate unanswered questions about highly emotionally significant issues well. The need to fill the void that these questions create is very strong, and all manner of solutions have been generated over the course of human history, most which have no basis in verifiable truth. All that matters is that the belief performs the function of satisfying the basic human need for a definition of reality. This need is a species wide universality and forms a major basis for social organization. We arrange ourselves into groups, or tribes, based on common, or group wide accepted beliefs. Belief systems then define us as tribes and as such are linked to survivability. They cannot be separated from our biology.

If we evolved both culturally and biologically to use beliefs as a major component of human social organization, then any attempt to remove this component from society should be difficult. Indeed, it's essentially impossible. Beliefs form the basis of both individual and societal identity and to remove them would yank out our humanity. We cannot be machine-like. This is the conundrum modern people face with the advance of science. We identify ourselves with our beliefs, and science continuously challenges our traditional beliefs, which then challenges our identities.

When modern anthropologists examine the beliefs of indigenous tribal people or study the beliefs of the past, they refer to them as "myths." The word "myth" carries a connotation of a falsehood. We think this way because our advanced technology shows that these myths are not empirically verifiable or they contradict known principles of science. Our technological might has only existed for a few centuries. Human beings have been engaged in myth creation for probably at least 40,000 years or as soon as we had the cognitive abilities to do so. Until the last few centuries, humans did not have the scientific means to dispel these ancient myths. So for virtually the entire cognitive history of our species, unverifiable, illogical, emotionally satisfying beliefs have formed the foundation of explanations of reality, which in turn form the foundation of human culture. The poetry of mythology and the legends of beliefs are an essential component of the human psyche. The story, the myth, the tale, the legend, the gospel, the scripture are just as natural and essential a component of our humanity as is our physiology. They are a major element of the evolution of our consciousness and cognition. We need the poet, the soothsayer, and the prophet just as much as we need the scientist. Nature or God or natural selection or whatever you want to call it made us this way. These are very powerful forces that shape human behavior and worldwide events. It is essential that these dominant forces that heavily influence our minds be well understood in order to move civilization forward. Maybe this is why history keeps repeating itself. We don't understand why we do what we do, so we keep doing the same things over and over again. War demonstrates this.

Most of the recent so called anti-God books make basically the same argument, which is that if superstitious religious beliefs were replaced with rational thought, the world would be a better place (Harris, 2004; Dawkins, 2006; Dennett, 2006). They all blame the terrible things that people do to each other in the name of religion.

But rational thought can never function as a replacement for beliefs, because beliefs satisfy emotional needs, not rational ones. Moreover, the mechanism for violence enacted in the name of religion is actually tribalism, which utilizes religion as a means of group identification. This provides a reasonable explanation for why we keep killing each other in the name of God. The problem we as a species need to work on is tribalism.

How do symbols interact with belief systems? Symbols function as very powerful representations of beliefs. Since symbols are not precisely defined with language, they can have different meanings for everyone who views them. Each one of us effectively "personalizes" what any particular symbol means (O'Shaughnessy, 2004). They become a part of us, a component of our own identity. Symbols can evoke tremendously powerful emotions that words can only superficially describe. What words can capture the feelings one has when witnessing images of American soldiers liberating a Nazi death camp or a lynched teenage boy hanging from a noose? Everyone sees the same image, but it means a little something different to all who view it. The intensity of the debate concerning the display of religious symbols, the flag, the Pledge of Allegiance, the Ten Commandments, and others is caused by this personalization of the symbol as a means of defining individual identity. To tarnish the image that one might have for a particular symbol is worse than a slap in the face. It rips at the very essence of who we are, or at least who we think we are. It's powerful stuff and should not be casually bantered about by politicians and pundits seeking power or wealth. They are playing with deeply rooted psychological forces that for many lie outside the realm of rational moderation. This is like yelling fire in a crowded theater, a very socially irresponsible thing to do. This reaction is again not a matter of intelligence but of emotion, our tribal emotions.

Self-Identity and Tribes

There is a psychological aspect to all of these arguments
that we need to explore. The behaviors people display are
usually enacted to satisfy motivations that are generated
by incentives, such as needs and desires. In the case of
tribalism, people organize themselves into groups based
on common belief systems for reproductive fitness, basically to stay alive, but there must be a psychological component to the motivation as well because people just don't
need to join groups, they want to. The motivation must be
strong, because people have been displaying this behavior
all over the world for many tens of thousands of years. If
the motivation is universal, does it have something to do
with reproductive fitness? When people join a group, are
they consciously or unconsciously doing so to have more
babies? Is there a desired outcome or goal that people seek
from group membership? If so, is that outcome just to survive? If that were true, then people would just join groups
that have the highest population growths and reproductive rates. Do Democrats have higher survival rates then
Republicans? Do Kantian rationalists have higher birth
rates then students of Marx? Joining a group is a conscious
decision. It may be an irrational choice, and it is always an
emotional choice. A primary motivation for joining a group
that necessarily entails embracing the group's ideology is
an emotional motivation, and a component of that motivation is the generation of self-identity.

A person's beliefs literally define the essence of an
individual's self-identity. As conscious, sentient beings,
we are the sum total of our wants, needs, and desires. But
what do we want, and what do we desire? How are those

factors defined? We want and desire things that we value. But what defines the things we value? Again, we are back to our belief systems. They define what it is that we value. So how do we choose what belief system to believe? We choose to believe things that are emotionally significant. Why does one person chose to believe that the world is 5,000 years old and another chooses to believe the world is close to five billion years old? Because the 5,000-year figure and related concepts are more emotionally significant to one individual, and the five billion-year figure and its related concepts are more significant to the other. They are two different people with different heritable and environmental, or cultural, experiences. So who we are as differentiated from others is largely determined by our beliefs. Our beliefs literally define us. They form the backbone of our self-identity. This is why people tend to get so terribly upset when their beliefs are challenged or not respected. Our beliefs and their rituals are not just things we do; they are essentially what we are at the most personal and intimate level. Understanding that essential part of human behavior explains why symbols, values, and beliefs are so important in politics. Group affiliation, group identity, forms a huge part of self-identity. Symbols and the beliefs they represent are the expressions of both the group and self- identity. Their absence or misuse tears at these identities, which can cause great consternation and anger. The Religious Right and conservatives in general have pushed this issue to the forefront of the political world. I'm not sure if this is a good thing or a bad thing, but it certainly is a human thing, a tribal thing. Maybe this is why people often say, "All politics is local." Nothing is more local than a person's self-identity. From my observations, the political right makes much more frequent use of and stresses the importance of symbols than the left.

If the essence of who we are is defined by what we believe, then this must be the mechanism the mind uses to define itself to itself. Conscious existence necessitates a definition of reality, and our own consciousness is a part of that reality. The concept of self-identity is, then, the foundation of consciousness.

This line of reasoning indicates that if beliefs form the basis of self-identity, then formal religion functions as an essential component of the self. That is to say, religion is a necessary part of being human, just like having a brain. The advanced intelligence of humans gives us the power, the ability, to ponder and question our own existence. These questions and their answers are required for the establishment of our self-identity. Our intelligence drives human culture to create a class of explanations, a genre of solutions that attempt to solve the mysteries of existence, which is religion. In other words, we don't create religion because we can; we create religion because we have to.

Deity worship is not a requirement for being human. It is a set of solutions that answer the questions of existence and being, and those solutions may be scientific or philosophical. The set of beliefs may even center on a belief in nothingness. It is also not to say that any particular religion is correct or not. The "correctness" of the belief is related to how well it satisfies the need for concepts of existence and being for any particular individual. This argument does not prove or disprove that there is religious truth, but it does establish that the genre of solutions that encompasses religion satisfies a basic human need, and that need is the development of self-identity. This is why religion has such tremendous power over us and is such a huge component of politics.

Self-Identity is largely derived from group identity meaning that the groups we belong to define us to ourselves. This process of identification through group culture must then be a natural process. It is the result of the marriage between the biological and cultural evolution of the human mind. This marriage gives my theories much more power. It provides a two-phase interactive system that reinforces itself. In engineering parlance, this is a system of positive feedback. We join groups to stay alive, and we use the group's beliefs to generate our self-identity. This belief-based identity then provides additional emotional significance to the group's beliefs, which provides additional motivation to support the group. What I'm describing is a trap of human thought processes that causes emotion to supersede logic, which is rooted in the beginnings of human group development. The trap is extremely powerful, and people don't realize they are affected by it, because their thoughts operate from inside it. It's a part of our natural mental "operating system," and the operating system can't see itself operate. We can't see the forest for the trees. Highly educated people are not immune from the trap. Acquiring a bunch of advanced degrees does not shatter the trap, because the trap is based on emotion, not reasoned thought, and our emotions are the dominant force controlling our thoughts.

A reasonable question is, "How could such behaviors have become so widespread and universal?" This could have easily happened.

Recent genetic studies indicate that the entire modern human population descended from a single African population. These ancient humans were under extreme pressure to survive, because from about 135,000 to 70,000 years ago, Africa experienced a series of severe droughts that depopulated the continent to as few as 2,000 individual humans. Surviving bands migrated to and coalesced in northeast Africa. (Behar et al., 2008) It was our ancestors' "last stand" against nature, and, fortunately for us, they made it through. This occurrence is extremely significant to my theories. It indicates that all of humanity was subjected to the same extreme environmental pressures for tens of thousands of years. Natural selection would have acted on those populations and weeded out the weak or less suitable to survive under these difficult conditions. Only those populations that possessed the necessary physiology and behavioral strategies to combat the stress would have survived. Our ancestors of this period probably did not have much physiological diversity, if any. Racial diversification would not even occur for several tens of thousands of years. The edge that the survivors had was most likely the strategy and behavior they employed. This means that how people organized themselves into groups and the strategies of interaction they employed made the difference in who passed their genes on to the next generation and who did not. I view this period like a pressure cooker of human evolution. It may even have contributed to the advance of human intelligence, as the smartest people would have a greater chance of figuring out how to stay alive.

If organizing people into cooperative groups enhanced survival, this period certainly would have put that theory to the test. Those who developed strategies that utilized the group, the "us," to their best capabilities were the ones that made it through. Natural selection would have concentrated the necessary genetic physical and behavioral traits in those populations as well as any cultural systems associated with them. The level of cultural sophistication from this period is unknown as is the formalization of any belief systems, but it is fair to assume that there was at least some cultural activity. If the feature exists, even in low levels, then natural selection can concentrate it. Any intensification of the concept of the "us" in human society would have necessarily intensified the concept of the "them." Over long periods of time, this intensification would have increased because of its positive affects on reproductive fitness.

I have presented a logical and plausible scenario for the development of a mechanism that allowed belief systems to function as a primary means tribal identification, which was then installed in the entire human race as an innate behavior, or at least an innate tendency for that behavior in the mind. This, then, would provide a very powerful mechanism in the brain that could alter the way we think, and that's why we keep killing each other in the name of group beliefs all over the world.

Yes/No Decisions

Belief systems are used to determine the "in" group and "out" group. It's "us" or "them." This decision is made on an all-or-nothing basis. A person can't be half a tribe member just as a person can't be half pregnant. The decision is always outputted in a yes/no format, and the basis for it is made by determining if the individual follows the tribal belief systems. But how did this property originate? There is a biological basis for it. So let's go back to evolution and see how all this may have come to be.

Emotions are automatic responses to stimuli. Emotionally based decisions in more primitive life forms are implemented in the form of an impulse response. Their original purpose was to function as a mechanism of survival. See a predator, run like hell. No time to think about it. See food, eat it. See a prospective mate, approach and try to mate. All of these decisions are based in a yes/no format. Human beings have similar physiological structures in our brains as animals that rely primarily on the impulse response, and they serve a similar function. They are there to keep us alive.

Humans also have additional structures that give us greatly enhanced mental abilities. The pre-frontal cortex is where the seat of consciousness resides, the sense of the "I," the self (Goldberg, 2001). When an emotional response is activated, a corresponding physiological response is triggered in the body. The heart can start pounding, or breathing is increased, for example. The pre-frontal cortex monitors these responses and reports to the "I" module that you are happy, sad, afraid, etc. So it is not the emotion we are aware of, it's the physiological response in the body created by the emotion that we sense that causes us to be aware of the emotion (Carter, 1999).

The emotional structures, sometimes referred to as the limbic system, have about ten times the neural pathways leading out into the cortex as in reverse. This is an indication of its importance to survival.

When an emotional response is triggered, the physiological response is practically immediate. Chemicals are secreted, hormones and neurotransmitters that cause physiological changes in the body. Then the conscious centers kick in. The thinking part of the brain begins to analyze the situation to see if it's a false alarm and how serious the problem is. If the problem is not serious, more chemicals are secreted and electrical signals are sent into the limbic system to reverse the impulse and restore the brain to a resting state. The emotional impulse reaction is basically what a teenager is: a walking, talking impulse machine. In fact, the apparatus of impulse control is not fully formed until we reach our mid-twenties. There is an insulation that covers the neurons called the myelin sheath, which is a fatty substance that literally provides insulation for the electrical signals transmitted through them. The insulation is not fully formed until we reach our mid-twenties. The voice of age is most certainly the voice of reason.

There are two things required to reverse the impulse: time and training. The more training the mind has in dealing with the particular stimulus, the quicker it can regain control. This is the basis of wisdom, which is essentially pattern recognition (Goldberg, 2006). Law enforcement officers, doctors, firefighters, and others that deal with rapid life and death decisions must have rigorous training to develop the pattern recognition to deal immediately with these types of critical problems. Our biological programming is not to reason through a crisis. The natural response is to run like hell or fight like hell. Life experience and education are the allies of reason. Youth, or very limited experience, and lack of education are the enemies of reason. That's why it's always a good idea to put a well-schooled individual with a rich and varied life experience in a position of power instead of an impulsive, uneducated, immature person.

The case I'm making is that resident in the mind is the emotional impulse response, a powerful and dominating feature that outputs decisions into a yes/no format.

We are constantly confronted with complicated situations that we do not fully understand. We often rely on belief systems, such as superstitions, to provide us with solutions, because we often have few other tools to use.

The output of this process of applying a belief to solve a problem is necessarily constrained to a yes/no format, because the belief is applied or it isn't. If this were not true, then answers would primarily be more in the form of a proportional response, a little of this and a little of that. This is not what I observe people doing. Decisions greatly tend to coincide with the directives of a belief. This is not laziness, but rather a result of our biological programming. It's a matter of efficiency. In life-threatening situations, there is no time to postulate. A decision must be made immediately. The first and foremost decisions we make as a species concern staying alive, and nothing is more emotionally significant than survival. We do what we believe will keep us alive. This is why our minds are wired to produce an initial yes/no response. No time-consuming reasoning is required, just the acceptance of a belief.

The ritual is a problem-solving device in that it is performed in order to produce a desired outcome. The ritual is either performed or it is not, which also forces the decision process into a yes/no format, because it is believed that the desired outcome will not be achieved unless the ritual is performed. The ritual is then a ready-made solution defined by a belief system. Rituals form a catalog of solutions for us to access. Belief systems then provide us with a cookbook of answers. The recipes in the cookbooks were initially "how to stay alive," which gives them the highest degree of emotional significance. Since the initial use of these recipes was to enhance survival, natural selection could operate on them and install this method of problem solving as an innate feature of the mind. This creates a reasonable possibility of the linkage of biology to methods of problem solving.

If the emotionally based yes/no decision process is

fundamental to animal behavior, then logic and reasoned thought would have to be additions to this base. They are features that must have emerged more recently and function on top of the base of yes/no decision-making. It takes education and training to access the logic and reason features of the mind fully and break this cycle to consider alternatives or new combinations of solutions. Otherwise, we simply react emotionally and default to the belief system-driven yes/no means of solving problems.

There is another aspect of the emotional response that must be integrated with yes/no thinking. Our brains are constantly bombarded with sense data. Our eyes see every crack in the floorboards. Our skin feels the shoes on our feet. Our sinuses notice every bit of breath that passes through. But most of the time, we are unaware of this information. Why?

The primary function of the brain is to keep the animal alive. That means eating and not being eaten. Our minds have evolved to respond to sense data that is survival critical. See a leopard in a tree, run away now. See a blade of grass blowing in the wind, who cares? Our minds must be able to segregate information into critical and non-critical categories on an automatic basis. This is absolutely essential to the survival of the animal. Any creature that can't do this will become easy prey, which will reduce its chances of reproduction and minimize this characteristic in its respective species. Creatures that can successfully make the segregation will most likely survive and concentrate the information segregation characteristic in its population.

The emotional attribute of this information and its direct connection to survival cause it to be processed by our minds in a yes/no format. This feature of the mind is a product of evolution and is common throughout the animal kingdom. Zebra sees lion, zebra runs. Lion sees zebra, lion pounces.

The survival fight/flight response is a time-critical response. There is a limit to the rate that brains can process information. The only way the run/fight response can be efficiently utilized in time-critical situations is if non-essential information is filtered out, thereby relieving the mind of unimportant processing so it can focus on keeping the animal alive. This is exactly how our minds function. The information we first process is survival-related. This necessarily implies a filtration process of sense data. There is no other way to get rid of the non-critical information unless it is filtered before being processed.

Since human minds possess this feature, it also seems to affect problem solving and perception. I have observed many, many times that when people engage others in a heated exchange, no one listens to anyone. Any information that contradicts what either party is arguing, or believes, is ignored. As far as the combatants are concerned, the information does not exist, and so they simply don't respond to it. People don't listen to each other, because they really don't hear each other. Information that supports their beliefs is emotionally significant and is processed. Everything else is thrown away.

Here is an example of how this characteristic affects me. In my studies of human behavior, I tried to understand some basics of microbiology. I tried to read a little about the biochemistry of cells to understand better how behavior is implemented in creatures at the cellular level. I just hate chemistry. I did in high school and still do today. When I would try to read this information, it just went right through me. Next thing I knew, I was five pages farther into the book and didn't even realize I had turned a single page. I kept trying and always had the same result. My mind just filtered it out like it wasn't there. Chemistry is just not emotionally significant to me. I can't learn it, not because the concepts are too difficult for me, but because I plainly don't care.

This example is very revealing of these processes, because I love science, all kinds of science, and have since I was a little boy. So why don't I like chemistry? The answer must be rooted in my worldview, how my mind defines reality. All of us must have some basis of forming a conception of reality. I view the happenings of the natural world as a result of the laws of nature, and these laws form a type of Ten Commandments for my mind. They establish a basis of my reality. By understanding these laws, nature is revealed to me, which gives these laws the highest emotional significance to my mind. They form a belief system that I use to define the world. If I can master these laws, then I can explain things that I experience. If I can understand these relationships, I can calculate or predict what any specific effect will be. My problem with chemistry as a discipline is that it does not appear to my mind to fit my worldview. It appears to me to be an assortment of specific effects, instead of an overarching principle that defines specific effects. Consequently, my mind views it as just noise.

My problem with chemistry is a great example of why teaching is so difficult. Even for a man that loves science, an entire component of that field is locked out to me, because of my emotions. The task of the teacher is to present the information so that it is emotionally significant to the student. Otherwise, it's "game over." The student will just filter it out and not respond to it. The only way to accomplish that feat is to integrate the information into the student's worldview so it attains a degree of emotional significance. Since everyone has a different worldview to some extent, teaching is really hard to do.

This filtration effect has a huge impact on yes/no thinking. We filter out information that is not emotionally significant, which is usually anything that contradicts what we want to believe or has no inherent emotional significance. What we do register and respond to is information that supports our beliefs. We then create a polarized view of the world: "I'm 100% right and you are 100% wrong because my data is 100% correct and your contradictory data does not even exist, therefore my position cannot be challenged and is a perfect argument." My beliefs, my worldview, are then completely secure no matter what. The stimulus that triggers these behaviors is the emotional significance of the belief to the individual. The more significant, the greater the intensity of the filtering response. This is the embodiment of yes/no thinking. Tribalism and its hold on how our beliefs shape our thoughts is the villain here. It causes us to adhere to our beliefs, or should I say, our sacred beliefs, because they define us, our tribe, and cause us to ignore completely contradictory information.

As the result of these arguments, I have concluded that when belief systems are used as a determinant for some logical requirement, the output of the process will naturally be in a yes/no format. That is, our biological programming drives us to output solutions in a yes/no or all or nothing format. We create solutions that satisfy our worldview in the form of belief "A" or not "A." The more educated and sophisticated mind creates solutions in the form of part of "A," part of "B," and maybe a little of "C" or some other belief system. Only an educated and developed mind can consider the possibility of solutions in a format that utilizes components from a variety of belief systems. I want to emphasize the difference between an educated mind and a trained mind. An individual can be highly trained, acquire a Ph.D. and still not be educated in that their responses and worldview are still locked in this tribal morass of information filtration and yes/no thinking. The mark of a truly educated person is one who can break out of this pattern and embrace intellectualism, the pursuit of truth and wisdom. This is much harder to do than would initially appear, because it requires throwing off the yoke of our tribal programming and replacing it with reasoned thought. We have to become less emotional, less human, to understand our humanity fully. A difficult task indeed.

Cognitive Dissonance

Integrated into the filtration process is the action of cognitive dissonance. Dissonance theory is an established principle of the mind, something real scientists study (Tavris and Aronson, 2007). It functions as the glue for my theories. But what is it, and how does it work?

During the Bush/Kerry debates, if a Bush supporter were asked about the outcome of a particular debate, he would likely respond, "Bush creamed Kerry. It was a massacre." If a Kerry supporter were asked about the outcome of the same debate, he would likely respond, "Kerry creamed Bush. It was a massacre." Each observer would also probably ask, "Why can't that other guy see it my way? What's wrong with him? He must be nuts!" Now, how could two people view the exact same event and see two completely different outcomes? How is this possible?

We think we are these rational, sophisticated beings, but

we are not. We are controlled and ruled by our emotions.

Not long ago, a business associate of mine told me, "Facts don't matter." His case was that facts could be manipulated to mean anything you want them to mean. I think he was confusing propaganda with factual information, but he opened up my mind to an important principle. He was right. Facts really don't matter. Here's why.

Dissonance theory teaches us that the mind reinterprets our sense data, everything we see and hear, into a form that satisfies our emotional needs. We hear what we want to hear and see what we want to see. We filter out information that contradicts the way we want to believe the world really works, such as, "the earth is 5,000 years old," or "all big corporations are evil." The believer filters out information that contradicts these statements.

Dissonance is even worse than this. We rewrite our memories to construct an experience of reality that pleases us. When we witness congressional hearings, we see people testify about events that happened months ago. When their testimony completely contradicts what actual physical recordings of the events establish, it looks as though they are the biggest liars on the planet. Some are most assuredly lying, but most are probably convinced they are telling the truth. Their minds have rewritten the past into a form that pleases them. They may well believe that their side didn't do anything wrong, and that those other guys caused all the problems. This is why, if you are ever involved in a dispute or potential dispute, you should write it up immediately. The longer you wait to give your side of the story, the more time your mind will have to rewrite history, and so will your opponent's. Our recollections of past events are essentially subject to change without notice. This characteris-

tic is used by the mind to push beliefs into a form
we will accept.

In short, we react emotionally instead of rationally to
just about everything. It's all about how we feel about
things, not what we know about things. We constantly rear-
range all the information that enters our brains into a form
that pleases us emotionally. It's a wonder that anyone ever
learns anything. The key here is that the rearrangement
is governed by what any particular individual requires to
satisfy their particular emotional needs.

But what need is that? Our belief systems define the
way we look at the world, politically speaking, it's our
worldview. For example, many years ago, an Iraqi friend
at work told me, "Bruce, you see all those TV commer-
cials for McDonalds hamburgers and Coca-cola. They are
examples of how the Jewish conspiracy is trying to take
over the world." I replied, "But I don't see anything there."
Then he said, "But you don't know what to look for." That
nails it. This is a great example of how dissonance works.
The Iraqi was convinced that something is there even when
nothing is there. He finds what he is looking for wherever
he looks for it because he wants it to be there. The
evidence has to be omnipresent, because the belief
system says so.

Dissonance is so strong that we manufacture facts as
needed. The world really is what we believe it to be, no
more, no less, as defined by our belief systems. There is a
direct link between belief systems and cognitive dissonance
in that the belief system defines what the world is, and dissonance causes the world to appear to be the way the belief
system defines it.

The action of dissonance is silent. We are not aware that it affects us. We see it in others, such as the example with the Bush/Kerry debates, but we don't see it in ourselves. This raises some interesting possibilities.

Let's look at this from a functional perspective. We have a property that all humans possess. It acts automatically and unconsciously. If we all have it and it functions on automatic pilot, then that indicates a strong possibility that it is an innate part of our natural biological programming, like being attracted to the round face of a baby. Or it could be culturally transmitted universally with the net affect the same as if it were biologically programmed into us. Dissonance affects what we know by altering how we know it. Ultimately, how we know things must be a combination of genetic and environmental factors that are resident in the mind. As we grow from infancy, our minds develop the skills of processing information. If following tribal beliefs were necessary to stay alive, then some learned response always to accept as true whatever those tribal beliefs were could have been culturally transmitted universally. Otherwise, people would start dying off. This does not explain the condition of the modern world, where following tribal beliefs are not necessary to stay alive, and yet everyone still suffers from cognitive dissonance. I am inclined to believe that biology is the source.

Dissonance is a component of self-identity, which is the basis of conscious existence. The explanations that people use to generate self-identity possess the highest degree of emotional significance. Doubting one's own existence generates a tremendous amount of anxiety. Since dissonance operates on the emotional significance of information, it stands to reason that any information processed by the mind relating to definitions of identity is strongly acted upon by cognitive dissonance. This is why people believe what they want to believe, particularly regarding group-based beliefs, such as religion and politics. Our core emotional nature prevents us from being rational.

Since innate behaviors are installed by natural selection to improve reproductive fitness, then in what possible way could cognitive dissonance have been installed as an innate component of our minds?

If being a member of the tribe meant staying alive, and following tribal beliefs meant being a member of the tribe, then following tribal beliefs meant staying alive. This relationship links the following of tribal beliefs and reproductive fitness. Such a link is a property that can be acted upon by natural selection. Cognitive dissonance would be such a property.

If the non-followers of belief systems were kicked out of the tribe and perished, then people that followed the belief systems would be the ones to survive. Any inheritable traits that encouraged following tribal beliefs would tend to be passed on and concentrated in the population. I have no theories as to the ultimate origin of dissonance, but any mental process that improved tribal unity would improve reproductive fitness, allowing it to be selected for. It is so important to be a part of the tribe that our minds may have been programmed by natural selection to believe and accept as true whatever the group beliefs dictate. If this were not the origin of dissonance, it was likely one of its earliest applications. Evolution is an efficient process and will harness existing structures and behaviors and then modify them if that improves fitness in a new niche, such as bipedalism in humans when quadruped pelvic structure was modified. Using belief systems as an improved cultural system for group identification certainly could have been one of those new niches. So the possibility is very real that dissonance was solidified in the mind through natural selection by improving tribal unity, even though its ultimate origin may have came from some other evolutionary process.

Follow the Leader

If there is a link between tribal leadership and survival, then natural selection could operate on it and select for the characteristics of that link. In what way could this link have manifested itself? How does leadership increase survival?

Life is full of mysteries. We constantly have to make decisions about things to which we cannot possibly know the answers. We have to guess. We rely on leaders to guide us through these unknown perils. It's a matter of survival. Think of it this way. Today, we find terrorism to be just that, terrifying. The thought that death could strike without warning at any time, at any place is indeed a frightful thought. Now turn, the clock back 20,000 years. How do you think it felt to live in a world full of powerful predators and rival groups that could take life without warning at any time? Sounds like a lousy deal to me. Maybe back then people were numb to it, because their world was full of sudden death. Maybe not. If I were to venture a guess, I would say that the sight of a lion killing a group member was, to say the least, traumatic. I can't imagine how horrifying it must have been when, all of the sudden, a raiding party swooped in and started killing people and stealing females, even for people with more primitive minds.

The need for government increases as groups expand. Intensification feeds on itself, and groups keep growing until they reach resource depletion. As groups become larger, more sophisticated organizational structures are required, and some form of leadership is required to maintain stability and order. Leadership necessarily implies a formal means of social regulation. Otherwise, there would be no mechanism with which to lead.

Government involves a distribution of political power. This necessarily requires some kind of selection process for leadership positions. Whom do we select, and why? Or does the leader select himself and take power? Is tribalism involved? Boy, is it ever. Let's first take a look at the animal kingdom. What kind of animal leads the tribe?

Usually, it's a male. Most animal societies are patriarchal. Bonobos are an exception and are matriarchal (De Waal, 2005). They don't kill each other like male dominated societies do. Chalk up a win for estrogen. The male leader is usually the biggest, toughest, strongest animal in the group. He gets most, if not all of the breeding opportunities. If there are squabbles in the group, he puts them down. If the group is threatened, he leads the charge to fight. The group follows behind him as they traverse the countryside. If he leads them into danger very often, there won't be a group left. They'll become dinner for predators. Wait a minute. Take out the breeding rights, and this sounds like I am describing the ideal candidate for President of the United States! Are we just like a band of apes? Unfortunately, I think there is a lot of truth to that statement. What is it that we want in our leaders? How does the tribal response affect the selection process of picking a leader?

During the period of our history when the band was commonplace, leadership within the group was primarily a matter of personality and prestige (Johnson and Earle, 2000). Life has taught me that most people aren't leaders. They want someone to follow. Only a small percentage of the population is what I call "natural leaders" and is referred to in the literature as "aggrandizers." They have the personality and attitude to take charge, or at least try to take charge. It appears that aggrandizement has its roots in our ancient past. As others have written, evolution may have a part in this formula, because, in order for society to remain stable, most people need to be followers to maintain the status quo. But society cannot move forward unless there are a few trouble-makers around that push the envelope and try to make improvements. If most people had that personality type, society wouldn't be able to hold together. So from an evolutionary view, it makes sense that the vast majority of people are followers.

At the next level of leadership at the local group level, the additional criteria of production, warfare, and beliefs or ideology would come into play. Production involves securing the resources and materials needed for survival, such as food. Individuals that lead and secure large amounts of food for the group obviously would be held in high regard. Success in warfare is also a highly desired characteristic for a leader. In a brutal world, groups not successful in combat would not be around very long. Keep us safe, great leader. Sound familiar? The third characteristic of ideology links beliefs to leadership, which ties them to centralized control. I have continuously maintained that beliefs define the tribe. Beliefs and systems of government are now intertwined. State religion is born. The leader, the chief, can use beliefs as a justification for actions and purpose. They can be used as an enforcement mechanism of societal control. The leader that embraces and projects the group's beliefs will acquire prestige and status as functioning as a conduit between the group and the supernatural forces that the beliefs purport to harness. Beliefs are now an integral component of power (Johnson and Earle, 2000).

As human societies became larger and more complicated, underlings, or lieutenants to the chief, would have been necessary to administer the business of the state, but they would have answered to the chief. Hierarchal management structures would have been developed as driven by the size of the state.

When reporters ask voters what kind of a person they want for President, one of the most frequent responses I hear is, "I want someone who is strong and honest." Let's analyze this statement. When they say strong, do they mean physical strength? Absolutely! Pair an imposing, tall, broad-shouldered, John Wayne-type next to a small, squirrelly nerd, and guess who will probably get the most votes. But strength means something else. It means strength of character. An honest person is someone who can be trusted. Our hypothetical voter is not addressing intelligence or problem-solving ability as a primary requirement. Yes, those are important issues, but not primary issues. Character issues are the ones that dominate. So how do we determine if a person is of strong character? Religion.

Piety has always been a marker for strength of character (Boyer, 2001; Atran, 2002). If a person stands up and proclaims themselves to be an atheist, the immediate reaction from most people would be that this person must be a no-good low-life. To reject the tribe's belief system, specifically religion, is to appear to be untrustworthy and dishonest. We think this way because the accomplishment of piety is a demonstration to the tribe that the individual has undertaken a great deal of personal sacrifice for no direct gain other than piety itself. The individual is a strict adherent to the tribal rituals and, therefore, its beliefs. Piety is a marker for trustworthiness and integrity, because the individual has endured many hardships to attain a high state of piety. It's a badge of honor. Here again, the tribal response controls how we think by providing a mechanism for character evaluation. The belief system is not only used to determine who's in the tribe, it is also used to determine who is the most trustworthy. High character is, then, a strong selector for choosing leaders. This is exactly how we behave today. By not professing allegiance to the tribe's prevailing belief system, a candidate for national office in the US has very little chance of being elected.

Security is another primary criteria we use for selecting leaders. The main reason I observed voters giving for re-electing George Bush in 2004 was there he would keep us "safe." During troubled times, security trumps all other factors. The Bush campaign was actually run on this very issue. Could there be a biological reason why we look to leaders for safety? I think so.

A centralized system of societal control is the most time-efficient means of directing policy. Dictatorships are not fair and just, but they are efficient. When the tribe is under severe acute stress, such being attacked, there is no time to sit around and discuss the matter. The longer it takes to mount a response to the stress, the more people will die. All military systems are structured around a system of centralized command and control for this very reason. A rapid, organized, and coordinated response is the most effective response. That's why when we fight wars, the first thing we try to do is take out the opponent's systems of command and control.

In response to acute stress placed on the tribe, such as a raid by other humans, a coordinated response would be more efficient and effective than having everyone running around in circles. It is reasonable to assume that, with the presence of a ruler, the ruler would give orders, especially when survivability is in question. Staying alive in a hostile environment was top priority, and it would stand to reason that the order giver was probably an expert in combat. He would have to be, or the tribe would not survive. The purpose of the orders would be to direct some kind of response to the threat. This type of ruler would be the warrior chief. During situations that are time-critical, centralized control is about the only way to mount an effective response, whether during combat or natural disaster or other similar time-critical, life-threatening situation.

Following the tribal leader meant participating in strategies with the intent of enhancing the tribe's survivability. These strategies were things the whole group did together for the good of all. Dissent would then be looked upon as impairing the tribe's ability to respond to stress, which would reduce survivability. We would call this treason today. In the modern world, we kill traitors. Do you really think people would have been more sympathetic to traitors in ancient times? No way! Tolerance is a product of advanced civilization where we respect the right to dissent. Any treasonous behavior back then most likely would have resulted in death, or at least expulsion. This would reduce the percentage of treasonous people over time by weeding them out along with their genetic characteristics. In the modern world, treason is very rare compared to other crimes. Any cultural system that improves reproductive fitness could be selected for, and any genetic traits that reinforce that cultural system will then become concentrated in the population. I submit that we expect our leaders to lead us to safety and that the motivation to do so is a tribal response. Not only that, we do what the tribal leader tells us to do. Dissent reduces the effectiveness of the response. Therefore, following the leader increases reproductive fitness. If this is true, then it establishes a link between a behavioral characteristic and reproductive fitness, which again can be acted on by natural selection and implanted in our minds.

Following the leader is such a powerful motivation that it actually dominated formal education for over 1,500 years. I am speaking of Aristotelian Scholasticism. The basis of this scholasticism is that Aristotle had everything figured out. He was the ultimate authority of science. The Catholic Church adopted the teachings of Aristotle as the foundation of science and employed them as a standard throughout the Holy Roman Empire. At that time, the Church controlled all the universities under their domain. Observable information, or empirical evidence, did not matter. Any information that contradicted the teachings of Aristotle would have been explained away with some reasoning, almost always invalid, that eliminated the contradiction. What mattered was that the principle held true, no matter what. This was maintained until Galileo figured out that observational evidence really did matter, which gave birth to the scientific method, and modern science was born. This was in the 17th Century.

This is all extremely tribal. We have a group of people, a tribe, which is primarily Catholic Europe. Membership in this tribe is delineated by a religious affiliation, which is defined by adherence to a rigid set of beliefs. The tribe has a chief, the Pope, who makes the rules. The tribe employs another set of rigid beliefs generated by another central authority, Aristotle, who could be regarded as the chief of the department of science. These beliefs, or explanations of reality, are given absolute authority and reverence, just like any other set of religious beliefs. They are not to be doubted and are treated as an article of faith. Reasoned thought was rejected as an explanation of reality and replaced with faith in the teachings of Aristotle. These behaviors are no different from any other tribal behavior inspired by a belief system. All tribal components are present and react in the same fashion. Rejecting the tribal beliefs can get a person in big trouble with the authorities. Look what happened to Galileo. The tribal based system of scholasticism actually controlled human thought for much of European history. The teachings of the leader take precedence over observation and reasoned thought. If you want answers, follow the leader. The leader will give you answers. The behavioral characteristic to seek and accept explanations from the leader is so strong that people mostly seek out leaders to follow, as opposed to leaders' convincing people to follow them. We need our heroes so badly that we manufacture them as required. This basic human need to seek guidance and explanations from leaders is so strong that it has given rise in the modern world to what I call the "cult of consultant worship," which has given the consultant great power in the marketplace. It seems as if hardly anyone in government or business can do anything without first hiring a consultant to tell them what to do. We hire, elect, and appoint people to positions of authority to make decisions for us, and the first thing they do when confronted with a problem is to hire a consultant. Even the leaders are looking for leaders to tell them what to do. We do this because of tribalism. It's a natural way our minds function.

There is another characteristic to following the leader I would like to explore, which is the way formal religion is structured. Formal religion is modeled in both the physical and metaphysical realms directly after the tribal system of strong centralized control with a primary leader, or chief, and a hierarchal distribution of power. In this case I am defining formal religion as moving past simple superstitious beliefs to be centered on deity worship.

It appears that many religious movements are centered on a primary leader figure. Committees don't start religions, individual people do. Committees, or disciples, may organize and spread the religion, but there is almost always a central originating figure. Examples would include Jesus Christ, Abraham, Moses, Muhammad, and Buddha. Submovements of these major religions have their own founders and leaders, such as Hasidic Judaism, various Protestant movements, Mormonism, etc. Point being, in the monotheistic religions of the Abrahamic tradition, there is always a central figure, a chief. All of these movements are centered on an individual, not just on an assortment of ideas. This is not just a coincidence. It is tribalism. The tribe functions around a central figure, a chief. The tribal leader often is the law and sets policy. The leader of a religious movement defines the belief system and sets the policy of the religion. The tribal chief and religious leader do the same things. They function in the same capacity, because they are the same. The major difference between the two is that the religious leader provides explanations of existence and being, which necessarily includes concepts of a metaphysical realm. The religious leader combines the functions of the tribal chief for both the physical and metaphysical realms. The addition of leadership in the metaphysical realm is an add-on to the basic survival functions of the tribal leader and is now required, because metaphysical beliefs are a more advanced cultural system needed to satisfy the desire to understand human existence.

The administration of religion over large population groups requires a hierarchal distribution of authority, just as large tribes have. There are bishops, cardinals, and priests and a central pope in the Catholic religion. All large religious movements have some kind of distribution of authority for efficiency of administration. The tribal structure of centralized control with a distribution of authority probably evolved because of its efficiency. Religious organizations are structured like tribes, because they are tribes.

Many metaphysical realms are also structured this way. The three major monotheistic religions, Judaism, Christianity, and Islam, all state that there is one, and only one God. But they also state that there are lesser supernatural beings. We call them angels, saints, and other names. The one God doesn't exist by himself in the metaphysical realm. God has underlings, or lieutenants, to assist in his tasks. He even has opponents, which we call variations of "Satan." Satan has underlings also.

The Romans were polytheists, but they spoke of God as a single entity. Their entity had underlings too. The sub-gods reported to the major god. Greek mythology is similarly structured. There is a history of hierarchal deity systems that date back long before the emergence of the three major monotheistic religions. The issue I raise is that the metaphysical components of religion are structured just as tribal systems are structured.

Political Ideologies and Tribalism

How are political ideologies related to tribalism and survival? Do they function as a type of religion, or is the other way around? As religions evolved, they essentially became systems of government. In fact, many modern religions are actually complete systems of government. The Old Testament and the Koran are complete codes of societal behavior. Nations are organized under them. This is one reason why we are having so much trouble in the Middle East today. Islam is more than a religion. It is a functioning system of government.

Many years ago, my Iraqi friend at work was showing me a map of the world. He outlined all the nations of the Middle East and North Africa and said to me, "Bruce, you see all these nations with their borders. It means nothing. There is only one nation. The nation of Islam." I never forgot those words. Of course, my friend was speaking globally of the Islamic world and non-Islamic world. There is no shortage of killing between the sub tribes of the Islamic world.

Why do Muslims keep calling Americans in Iraq "crusaders?" Because our stated mission is to install a liberal secular democracy in an Islamic country. But an Islamic nation can't be a liberal secular democracy. The two concepts contradict each other. To many Middle Eastern people, the Koran is their government, their way of life. Their religion is a theocratic form of government. To install a liberal secular democracy in Iraq is then viewed as a direct assault on their religion. This is why they call us crusaders. In this example, religion and political ideology are one.

As civilization continued to advance, particularly with the invention of agriculture, fewer and fewer people were needed to provide the basics of survival. This allowed for the division of labor and craft specialties. Because there was time to do other things, people could create goods that others wanted that essentially represented surplus resources. A regulatory apparatus had to be installed to administrate who got what, and how much they got, and who did what. Otherwise, there would be no way to establish order with an efficient means of production and distribution. We would call this "government." Political ideology then provides frameworks of who owns what, who gets what, and who does what. Who are the haves and have-nots. It determines how labor and resources are to be apportioned between tribe members both individually and collectively. Resources could also be diverted into what we now call public works projects. So the state now gets a share of the goods. Wealth distribution determines who has the resources to survive, especially during shortages and hence would be of the highest emotional significance. So political ideology determines the distribution of resources and is linked to survivability, just as religious ideologies are. An important distinction here is that frameworks of the distribution of wealth and power represent a more sophisticated cultural system than earlier religious ideologies, but in essence are still a component of survivability.

Political ideologies are belief systems that order and regulate social behavior. They are regulatory mechanisms based on belief systems and need to be followed in order for members of the tribe to survive. Their effect on the individual is that, if you want to survive and receive your share of resources and remain in the tribe, then you must follow the dictates of the regulatory systems. Political ideology then serves the same function as earlier religious belief systems and, in effect, has a similar impact on society. In fact, until the creation of the United States of America, virtually all nations had state religions. The two were literally one in the same.

Religious belief systems and political belief systems are intended to provide certain outcomes that satisfy desires.

Examples include the salvation of the soul, happiness in life, an ordered and moral society, and enough food to eat. These desired outcomes are actually solutions to problems. Public policies are enacted around various political ideologies with the intent of solving these types of problems.

Unfortunately, what often happens and what is supposed to happen don't quite match up. People don't come back from Heaven and tell us what the ride was like, so religious convictions cannot be physically verified. The economic status of peoples' lives, however, can be measured. When outcomes do not appear as intended, true believers of the ideology either ignore the outcome or blame the bad outcome on something else. Either way, the outcome doesn't change the true believer's mind. They believe just as intensely whether or not the outcome verifies the belief. This is exactly how we respond to religion. Religious leaders often state that reasoned thought is the enemy of faith. This is what they are talking about.

You People

In America, everyone seems to be a member of a group, and everyone else outside their group belongs to "you people." We often define "you people" by their racial heritage and by their belief systems. City people refer to rural people as "you people," and rural people respond the same way. Ditto for the religious to the secular and secular to the religious, the gun owners and the gun haters, and every other difference that people can point out about any other group. What happens is that these differences are used to justify superiority of one group over another. The gun lovers think they are superior to the gun haters because they love guns, and the gun haters think they are superior to the gun lovers because they hate guns. This is how it works.

Why? Why can't people accept that others are different and that's OK? Why are differences between population groups always reduced to an inferior/superior relationship. Tribalism is why.

I have maintained all throughout this book that belief systems define the tribe, and the purpose of the tribe is to determine whom to support and whom to kill. It's a lot easier to kill someone if they can be considered inferior and less than human. This is what we do during war. The enemy is reduced to a sub-species of animal that should be killed, just like pigs in a slaughterhouse (Smith, 2007). This is the foundation of wartime propaganda used by all nations. Any technique used to differentiate between population groups always ends up in a "you people" con- clusion, which is, of course, another example of yes/no thinking. My tribe is superior to your tribe because we do 'this" and you do "that," and the "this" is always superior to the "that," no matter what 'this" and "that' represent. We do this so we can justify killing and persecuting each other. The only way to eliminate "you people" is to homogenize society into one monolithic racial/cultural block, and that would take many centuries even if this were possible. Since this is essentially impossible to achieve, then we need to learn to all get along, but that can't happen unless we can talk about our differences. If we could talk to each other about each other, we might find out that we all have more in common than we realize. "You people" would start to turn into "we people."

Another component of "you people" is that it provides an outlet for hatred. All populations contain a substantial group of people that just aren't satisfied unless they have something to hate. If one enemy is dispatched, then anoth- er suddenly materializes that must be destroyed. I once had a Palestinian friend who told me that many of the people from his land just aren't happy unless they are at war with something. I'm sorry to say that this same type of thinking is a huge component of American politics. It is the essence of the politics of fear, which has been highly successful in the past for winning elections (though certainly not successful in governing). As a person who attended rough inner-city schools, I can confidently say that aggressive behavior is often displayed out of fear. The more dangerous the situation appears, the more aggressively people tend to act. The politics of fear is enabled by the perception of danger, which triggers aggressive behavior. This is the process we often use to justify killing other groups, and those that we kill are always "you people."

There is another aspect to "you people" that is subtler and fortunately doesn't involve killing. This is the desire for prestige. If there is one lesson that life has taught me, it is the universal desire for prestige. People want to be admired, respected, looked up to, and generally be held in high regard. Cultural systems have evolved that are used to satisfy these desires through the mechanism of grouping. I will call them "systems of exclusivity."

People constantly organize themselves into groups where common activities and/or beliefs are shared. The result of these groupings is a differentiation between the "in group" and the "out group." The grouping creates a sense of exclusivity, which results in feelings of superiority. Everyone outside of the group is de facto "you people." Professional societies, neighborhood associations, street gangs, country clubs, sports groups, etc., are all systems of exclusivity. They function as a means achieving prestige through their exclusivity. It does not matter if the individual joins the group to achieve prestige directly, or if the prestige is an unintended effect of group membership. In either case, prestige results by virtue of exclusivity. This is all extremely tribal. It's not that we just want to be together, but that our togetherness through exclusive groupings causes us to feel superior to others. This is what is tribal. To reinforce the validity of this statement, I ask the following question: when one group persecutes, denigrates, discriminates, tortures, enslaves, or murders members of another group, are these practices often accompanied by a sense of superiority? Yes, they always are. Whether or not the superiority occurs because of a need for justification of terrible acts is immaterial. Central to this argument is only whether the superiority accompanies the act, and it always does.

The Political Divide

The world appears to be divided into two main political factions. In other words, there are the secular/liberal type and the religious/conservative type. I want to emphasize that the term "religious/conservative" is not meant to be restricted to members of the Christian faith, but includes all faiths.

I see the division as one set of beliefs that restricts the range of permissible societal solutions and activities that is more exclusive of tribal membership, and one set of set of beliefs that employs a wider range of permissible activities and solutions that is more inclusive of tribal membership and hence less tribal. The demarcation is necessary, because conservatism as currently employed contains several major components that are self-contradictory, which I will elaborate further. A primary difference between conservatism and liberalism is the role of government in society, but that feature does not account for the contradictions. The more global differentiation I have chosen to use does.

The difference between these two is a rigid framework of social order, versus little or no framework of social order. The religious conservative mindset requires strict adherence to a rigid set of social regulations and sees the lack of regulations as just as great a threat to society as another opposing social structure. It views the difference between the two as either choosing social order with stability or decadence with societal collapse. The extreme liberal mindset replaces social regulation with relativism, which supports anything goes with everyone defining their own way of life and rejects overbearing social regulation, particularly with regard to what people do with their own bodies.

There is a division in the philosophy of constitutional law that breaks out along this very same argument. Conservative constitutional jurists believe that the U.S. Constitution must be applied in a very literal sense. There can be no interpretation or application beyond the explicit wording of the document. The intent of the Founding Fathers must be followed without any deviation. The Constitution is not a living document. Quite the contrary, it is static and only through the process of amendment can it be altered. The Constitution is the codification of a belief system. The followers of this belief system assign an almost supernatural characterization to the people who wrote it. These Founding Fathers are essentially deified, as their writings cannot be challenged. The followers, as true believers, assume they "know" the complete intent of the Founding Fathers. Their belief system gives them the ability to peer into the minds of men that lived over 200 years ago and understand their message without question. It's as if they claim to know the mind of God. They believe it is so, so it is so, as it is written.

Liberal jurists take a different approach. They view the Constitution as a living document. They hold the belief that the Founding Fathers were so gosh darn smart that they realized societies change over time. The Constitution was never intended to provide 100% coverage of all possible legal questions and conflicts, both present and future. It provides a framework for the legal system to operate under, necessitating the judiciary provide interpretation of the framework as new and unforeseen conflicts arise. Cultural norms change and adapt, primarily in response to advancing technology. The meaning of words changes over time as they are used in different ways with changing connotations. Language itself is dynamic, just like a living organism. Liberal jurists believe that we cannot possibly precisely know the exact intent of the minds of the Founding Fathers when they wrote that magnificent document. We can theorize and assume, but it is not possible to peer into the minds of men that have passed on centuries ago with absolute accuracy. There is always some range of interpretation, and it is the function of the judiciary to apply the Constitution best to the current needs of society. The Founding Fathers were men; they were not gods, and the works of men are never perfect.

Conservative and liberal religious views parallel the comparison between the conservative and liberal constitutional jurists.

The religious conservative views the Bible as being the exact word of God. There is no possibility for deviation and differing interpretations. All interpretations must be exactly literal. By following the exact dictates of the Bible, the true believer can peer into the mind of God. If logical contradictions are discovered, this is because our feeble human minds cannot comprehend awesome intelligence and purpose of God's mind. The Bible is static, it is permanent, and it never changes. The wording in the Bible must be followed exactly, or the individual cannot be a true believer. They believe it is so, so it is so, as it is written.

The liberal religious view takes a different approach. They maintain that Bible is not a book of prose, but a book of poetry, and was never intended to be interpreted literally. The Bible uses the instruments of metaphor and allegory in its poetic stories to teach timeless spiritual lessons about the world and how we should conduct our lives. This is the method of communication that God chose to speak to humanity through the divinely inspired words of men due to the timeless nature of poetry. The meaning of words and their connotations change over the course of thousands of years and should be viewed in a relative context. The changing meaning of words is further compounded by the fact that the words have been translated from ancient Hebrew to Aramaic to Greek to Latin to archaic English to modern English. Each translation alters their original intent. Men have heavily altered the content of the Bible as its contents were assembled. Sections and or gospels were either included or deleted. Some may have been permanently lost. Because of these factors, we cannot peer into the mind of God. We can only try to follow what God is trying to teach us. Because men had a huge part in the generation of the Bible, it is not a perfect document and thus cannot and should not be literally interpreted. The Bible is man's best attempt to worship and follow God. No works of man are perfect.

The parallel is incredibly similar. We have four groups of people behaving as if they were two sets of identical twins. The conservative pair uses a strict, rigid adherence to a belief system as codified in a revered document. The liberal pair uses a much less strict, more open and free-flowing adherence to the very same documents. Why?

This is yet another example of increased tribal behavior on the part of conservatives. Belief systems define the tribe, and strict adherence to the belief system demonstrates extreme tribalism. The more rigidly and exactly the tenants of the belief system are defined, the more precisely the followers of the group are defined. The rigid interpretation provides a strong line of demarcation that defines the "in" group and "out" group. The looser, more liberal set of definitions does not, because there is no clear line that cuts through the crowd and divides populations. The line curves, because the definitions are not clear. It all "just depends." The liberal view is therefore inherently less tribal, because it provides no clear division of groups. The rigid conservative view is much more tribal because it efficiently divides people into separate groups. The action of this division is the application of yes/no thinking inspired by a belief system further emphasizing its tribal nature.
I am arguing that strict adherence to belief systems is a product of tribal behavior. The essence of liberalism is the opposite. Liberals tend to apply a "whatever works" method of problem solving, while the conservative's method of problem solving must fall into an allowable domain of permissible solutions, primarily market-based solutions that exclude government participation, while the liberal domain of solutions includes government involvement as an acceptable component. The conservative method is then more restrictive and hence more tribal. My arguments are then defining liberalism as an ideology in so far as it is the absence of conservative ideology. Liberalism cannot be defined without conservatism. Allowing the government to participate in the social sphere is not so much a belief that it should, as much as it is the absence of a belief that

it should not. Contrary to propaganda constantly being spewed out by extremist media pundits, liberalism is not the desire to eliminate capitalism and the free market, but it does allow for the government to participate in fulfilling society's needs if it can do so with greater effectiveness and efficiency than market-based solutions.

When used to describe social behavior, the term "conservative" generally connotes people who are traditionalists. These are people who adhere to the status quo, the way we always have always done things. They desire to maintain time-honored procedures and practices. Nothing is wrong with that. But what defines what these practices are? The belief systems employed by the group provide these definitions. They define the practices that the traditionalists wish to maintain. So being a social conservative necessarily denotes a desire to follow the group's belief systems. But belief systems define the tribe. People who desire traditional social practices are then necessarily acting in a tribal fashion. The essence of social conservatism is therefore tribal.

Embracing social conservatism does not necessarily mean a person embraces political conservatism as it is currently employed. A person can have a strong desire for protocol, deportment, and etiquette and still strongly support publicly funded social security and labor unions. This is not a contradiction. We are all tribal to some extent. My arguments are centered on how tribalism affects the way we think, and people who are less tribal can be social conservatives and still accept inclusive, liberal politics. People who are strongly tribal cannot. The less tribal social conservative can accept the importance of marriage while still allowing for a legal union of homosexual couples (more inclusive), while the strongly tribal cannot (less inclusive).

A person can support liberal politics and not be in favor of turning society into a sewer of decadence, callous, and rude behavior. Cultural diversity is no excuse for cultural perversity. Political correctness is often used as means of glossing over perverse behavior in the name of individual freedom and inclusiveness, but such behavior is highly corrosive to society and should not be tolerated. This is what happens when not enough tribalism is employed. Society cannot hold together without decent, traditional, social practices and mores that form the basis of our social fabric, the weave that binds us into communities. However, this does not mean it is beneficial to society to employ practices that exclude others and treat them as if they are members of different tribes.

The very essence of liberalism is personal freedom, the liberty to do as one pleases without intervention or coercion from the state. The concept was conceived and developed during the period of enlightenment that culminated in the emergence of the United States of America in the form of a secular liberal democracy. Prior to that time, the nations of Europe were ruled by monarchies, or from my perspective, tribal chiefs. The ruler generally set policies in the interest of the state, not in the interest of the individual. A major theme of contemporary conservatism is to remove government from people's backs. It appears then that conservatives are really liberals. How can we account for this contradiction?

I see two major issues here. Both are tribal in nature. One is taxation, which will be addressed later. The other is the structure and complexity of modern society. Prior to the Industrial Revolution, American society was mostly agrarian and rural. Population densities were low, and most people lived in small communities. This is traditional and coincides with our biological evolution. With the advent of the industrial revolution two major shifts occurred. People moved into the cities that quickly grew into large metropolises, and advanced technology was introduced into everyday life. The rapid introduction of technology dramatically complicated the social fabric. It created many new ways of doing things and interacting with others. The cultural byproducts of technology require regulation, just as does other social behavior. The traditional social conservative understands the need for social regulation in order to maintain a functioning, ordered society, which is tribal. The left views this activity as a violation of personal freedom. The liberal views the need for regulation of the complex new systems brought on by advanced technology as necessary to maintain an ordered and functioning society, which again is tribal. The right views this activity as a violation of personal freedom. The two groups are employing similar tribal attitudes to different aspects of society. Why don't they view each other as members of the same group?

What we have here is the influence of yes/no thinking and filtration of information. Conservatives, being more traditional, view social regulation as being highly emotionally significant and the cultural components of the industrial age as falling under the purview of individual liberty. Liberals, being not so traditional, view the regulation of the components of the Industrial Age as being highly emotionally significant and social behavior falling under the purview of individual liberty. We all fall victim to the effects of tribalism. Both sides are suffering from the same effects of information filtration and yes/no thinking. Neither can see the positive implications of the other's position. It is the emotional significance of the position to the individual that determines which position is followed. Both sides are behaving in a tribal manner, but I would say that the conservative position is more tribal, because it is based in traditional social requirements that more effectively divide populations. This is exclusive. The liberal position is more concerned with the function of government that affects all group members equally and does not effectively divide populations. This is inclusive.

The geographic distribution of political ideology as currently shown by voting patterns reinforces this argument. Small town and rural America consistently vote conservative by a wide margin while large cities consistently vote liberal. Why such a division? Living in large metropolitan communities fosters a belief that essential services can only be supplied by government resulting from the size, complexity, and anonymity of large communities. Living in small communities, however, fosters a belief in independence from government intervention as their small size allows people to function as a cohesive community where they can provide essential services directly for each other. Anonymity is then replaced with personal relationships. This life style is more in agreement with our tribal roots and social evolution. The ecology of the small community causes them to not need as much government as big cities do. The differing ideology regarding the function of government between small and large communities is created by their social structure and that structure is mostly shaped by the size of the community. The size of the community drives the ideology.

The social organization of small communities is therefore, closer in function to our ancient tribal beginnings than are large communities because the application of government is a more recent addition to human culture. This causes people from small communities to view government intervention and regulation as an intrusion while people from large communities view it as essential to maintaining stability. This structural division in thought creates a greater intolerance for diversity of beliefs, primarily religious, in small communities. Small communities essentially function as independent tribes and the belief system defines the tribe. To reject the tribe's beliefs results in rejection by the tribe. Partisan politics operates on this very feature. Large communities, because of their size and complexity, cannot function in such a tribal manner. Consequently, they are generally more tolerant of different belief systems. This argument indicates that the voting patterns of America on a geographic basis are largely structural and therefore are essentially a permanent feature.

The liberal view of government is very similar to the model of an insurance company. Insurance works because most people need it only very infrequently and is structured to take advantage of this condition. If a very large body of people buys insurance, and only a small percentage needs to collect benefits in any given year, then the participants only have to pay a relatively low premium to cover the outlays. The system works because the many support the few on an infrequent basis as needed. To deny the validity of that statement is to deny the existence and viability of the insurance industry, which would be delusional, to say the least. I suggest that those who still think this argument is just a bunch of left wing socialist propaganda should investigate how much capital and maintenance expenses it would take to insure the value of one's home privately and compare that cost to one's annual homeowner's premiums. They will soon find that the "many supporting the few when needed" principal can be much less expensive to the individual when applied properly.

Most of us do just fine on our own for the most part.

But sooner or later, tragedy befalls almost all of us. Some-times these tragic occurrences are financially devastating, such as with long-term unemployment, illness, natural disaster, crime, fraud, and the like. If all of us pay an insurance premium in the form of taxes, then the combined financial might of all those premiums establishes a power-ful resource that can be used to assist with personal tragedy when infrequently needed. We call this resource our social safety net. The leading cause of bankruptcy in the U.S. is healthcare-related expenses, not buying big TV sets. Fur-thermore, we live in a highly technologically advanced civilization, and the cost of the infrastructure required to maintain it greatly exceeds the resources of even the super-rich. The premiums we pay in taxes finance this infrastruc-ture. In this case, the many support the many.

In a traditional hunter-gatherer band, the whole group has a vested interest in any individual. If some tragedy befell you, who would help you? Your parents? The guy down the street? Who's going to spot you a few hundred thousand dollars to tide you over, and how are you going to pay it back? There is no band or group that has a vested interest in your prosperity. Tragedies do occur in people's lives, and only the government has the resources to help, simply because with the absence of close-knit communities where individuals are interdependent upon each other, there are no alternatives. We do have the option to structure our society such that these types of programs are elimi-nated and just abandon people if they can't carry their own weight. We basically treat the mentally ill in this fashion. Most state mental hospitals have been closed due to budget cutbacks. There are currently only about 55,000 people residing in state mental hospitals and about 500,000 diag-nosed mentally ill housed in our prisons (PBS Frontline, *The New Asylums*, 2005). There are so many mentally ill incarcerated (about 20 to 25% of the prison population), that prisons are building mental health wards. This is what happens when helpless people are abandoned by society. They end up in jail or dead. What is ironic here is that the mental hospitals were closed to save taxpayer money, but it probably costs more to house the mentally ill in jail than in a facility designed for their needs where they can be supervised and get proper care. The taxpayer ends up spending more money and loses prison space that would be better suited to incarcerating violent criminals. For some reason, society views mental health as some kind of undesirable welfare program but sees building prisons as good for society, because it's an anti-crime position. Prevention is welfare and undesirable, while more expensive punishment caused by the lack of prevention is good for society and highly desirable. Go figure that one out.

If politics moves to the extreme left, totalitarianism again results. Instead of right wing fascist totalitarianism, such as Nazism, we get socialist totalitarianism, such as that used by Soviet Russia, which is just as bad. With totalitarian socialism, then yes, belief systems are again heavily involved in decision-making. These would include:

Everyone is equal, and no one should be allowed to outperform anyone else. If this were the best way to organize human society, we would all still be living in caves. Excellence must be encouraged for society to advance.

The government should regulate all aspects of society and equalize it. This is socialism taken to its extreme, which results in the minimization of personal freedom and the elimination of individuality.

This type of government requires a brutal dictatorship

for enforcement, just as with fascism. Soviet-style communism has nothing to do with Marxism, which is actually the elimination of government and formal centralized control. In 19th Century Germany, Marx blamed the tremendous inequality he observed between the masses of working class people and the wealthy aristocracy on capitalism. The goal of his system was social equality. Lenin used Marx's concept of social equality as a tool of propaganda with which he established a totalitarian dictatorship. His idea of social equality was keeping everyone dirt poor and under total control. I feel the need to mention this, because I have had many conversations with people aligned with the political right that believe that liberal policies are a direct path to Nazism. Hitler was not a socialist. Fascism is the complete opposite of communist socialism. The Nazis hated the communists and threw a few into their ovens. Hitler even invaded the Soviet Union, which greatly contributed to his defeat. Nazi totalitarianism is actually right wing politics taken to its extreme. Soviet-style communism as developed by Lenin has nothing to do with liberalism. Leninism is a system of absolute societal control enforced by brutal policies designed to instill complete fear of the government. Stalin murdered more of his own people than were killed by Hitler during World War II. Left-leaning American politics is a long, long way from Lenin and Stalin. Supporting the Social Security program is not an endorsement of installing a dictatorship where people get disappeared into dungeons. This type of misinformation is widely circulated by political pundits for political and economic gains. In other words, they make a lot of money doing it. It is very sad that so many Americans believe that their left-leaning neighbors are advocates of policies that can lead to Nazism, while right-wing extremists actually are and don't even realize it. Unfortunately, people that believe these falsehoods will probably never read this book.

The tenants of socialist communism are the result of following belief systems. These belief systems foster inclusion in that they force everyone into the group, while conservative belief systems are more exclusionary in that they restrict group membership. It appears then that conservatism is very tribal, as it requires strict adherence to belief systems that restrict tribal membership. As the political scale shifts to the left, belief systems become less rigid and more inclusive by allowing a looser and more open definition of tribal membership. As politics shifts to the extreme left, a strong adherence to belief systems is once again required to force everyone into the tribe. The means of forcing a 100% inclusion rate necessitates the elimination of individuality, which is accomplished through the use of belief systems that distort the reality that all people have different wants, needs, and desires. The extreme left attempts to eliminate the "them" by forcing everyone into the "us," while the extreme right attempts to make everyone "us" by simply eliminating the "them." Both ends of the political spectrum reach the same place where there is no personal liberty or individual freedom. They are both just as tribal.

Just as it is totally unfair and unrealistic to categorize conservatives as fascist Nazis, it is unfair and unrealistic to categorize liberals as individuality-crushing communists. Such individuals do exist on both sides of the political divide, but their existence does not and should not define the conservative and liberal movements. The extreme left's worldview of totalitarian socialism is not representative of liberalism in that it does not respect individual liberty. People on the right who make such claims are suffering from yes/no thinking and cannot generate a proportional response, and this is tribal in nature. Belief systems define the tribe, and conservatism is more tribal than liberalism.

I often hear rhetoric from conservative politicians that liberals want government to make decisions for people, while conservatives think that people should be left to make decisions for themselves. There is a huge difference between establishing societal regulations through the rule of law and having institutions making decisions for people. Because of the lack of traditional social influence on individual behavior, our society has implemented the rule of law to maintain social order. Yes, this limits the range of decisions people can make, but this is a necessary tradeoff required to maintain a civilized society. When I was a child, homeowners used to be able to burn their trash. If someone burned some noxious plastic or rubber, the stench and smoke throughout the neighborhood was horrible. We all suffered from it. The city banned open burning to eliminate that problem. Is this what is meant by the government's making decisions for people? What about regulations regarding child neglect or racketeering? What do you think would happen if all traffic speed limits were repealed? Having regulations that order society does not prohibit people from making decisions; it just limits the range to a level that maintains social order. There are a lot of people that make terrible decisions for themselves, and when they do, the public is put at great risk. Government has to make decisions for people like that to keep the rest of us alive. This is not socialism or a repeal of democracy, it's the reality of the human condition that our democratic system recognizes and which provides a good balance between individual freedom and the need for social order. If all people displayed 100% responsible behavior, 100% of the time, there would be no need for a legal code at all. Personal responsibility as a solution is only effective when people act responsibly, and that, I'm sorry to say, is not the case. People do things that endanger themselves and others, such as drunk driving, spouse-beating, speeding, child abuse, leaving loaded guns out in the open where small children can fire them, and so on.

If personal responsibility were the best solution to society's problems, and we examined a random grouping of people that swore allegiance to the conservative movement, we should expect to find a very low incidence of obesity, cigarette smoking, and alcohol abuse. There would also be many fit people who exercised vigorously at least five hours a week, because people that follow the edicts of the principles of personal responsibility should be expected to take care of their health. After all, isn't it in the best interest of the individual to maintain their health? This looks good on paper, but doesn't happen in real life. Personal responsibility is not a liberal or conservative issue' it's a people issue, and it doesn't always work, because people just don't behave in a responsible way all the time. People are not rational; they are emotional. Stick a chocolate cream pie in front of them and they eat the whole darn thing at once, never mind what political party they vote for. I am not in the least advocating the removal of the requirement of personal responsibility in a free and open democratic society. What I am advocating is recognizing that that the ethos of personal responsibility is no blanket cure for all of society's ills. There are other components that motivate behavior, specifically the sociological component.

People's behavior is affected by their environment. They tend to do things that society endorses or expects of them. The traditional way to look at individual behavior is that family values instill proper behavioral norms, and since society is made up of families, breakdowns in social norms are caused by breakdowns of family. Or is it the other way around? Do families decline because of the lack of support and increased pressure of modern life? Does the breakdown of the community cause the breakdown of the family? I recently viewed a video clip of Margaret Thatcher saying, "There are no societies, there are only families." Man, did she get it wrong! The reality of the situation is that families and societies cannot be separated in any kind of functional sense. The two are deeply intertwined and feed off of each other. The position of trying to treat society's ills with a family-oriented personal responsibility strategy just wont work without an integrated program of societal assistance. For example, a child can grow up in a bad neighborhood in a household with two loving parents that provide strict discipline and do everything right. The kid can start running around with the wrong crowd and, before you know it, start getting into trouble. Why did the child associate with the wrong crowd, especially if he were raised with all the right family values? Because that's the only crowd that lives there. The child was lost to the street. The child competes for success and status within his own environment (Pinker, 2002). This happens all the time and is devastating. In these kinds of situations, it is essential for government to provide assistance to the family to counter the negative influence of the street. There are simply no other options available to affect a workable solution. Another example is the criticism of Head Start. Children that have access to Head Start tend to do better in school in the early years, but by the time they reach about the fourth grade, academic performance falters. I have seen many conservative pundits use this as an excuse to justify that Head Start is a waste. The reason these kids falter is because they become lost to the street. Head Start does help them, but the support does not continue as they grow up. They are left to fend for themselves, and by the time they reach age ten or so, the street gobbles them up, and they are lost. The division in thought between the personal responsibility tactic and the social policy tactic is tribal.

Once again this is yes/no thinking. It's all or nothing, yet the only practical workable solution is a combination of both.

The entire position of treating the function of government as prohibiting individual decision-making is just another example of yes/no tribal thinking where the proportional response is ignored. This position is essentially an instrument of political propaganda intended to capture votes by appealing to a romantic notion of a freer, better time that never even existed in the first place, except in Hollywood movies.

The desired response of this propaganda produced by the right is purely emotional and is characterized in an "us against them" framework, where the "them" wants to take away the freedom of the "us." It portrays the government as some kind of enemy, the "them," which again is tribal. In a representative democracy, the "them" is "us." The tribal desire to target a "them" is so great that many people often lose sight of that reality. When it comes to taxes, the government is the evil "them" and is demonized. When it come to national security, the government is the "us" and is glorified, and anyone that doesn't join the celebration is unpatriotic or a traitor. It appears that the same groups that do most of the demonizing are the same ones that do most of the simultaneous glorifying. It's "Protect me and keep me safe, but don't tax me to pay for it." During the Reagan years, spending on national defense was dramatically increased, and, yes, that made the military stronger, but we didn't pay for it, and actually did the opposite and lowered taxes, which racked up huge deficits. President Bush has told us that the war on terror is the greatest conflict of the modern age and a tremendous threat to our freedom. Assuming this is true, then why hasn't a tax been levied to pay for the war on terror? Why is it that the citizenry gets a free ride while soldiers die? The excuse I often hear is that the additional taxes will inhibit economic growth. Of course it will! War is horribly expensive. That's the whole point of not waging war unless it is absolutely necessary. If we can't afford it, and we don't have to do it, then we shouldn't do it. Check your history books. Empires have collapsed under the burden of constantly waging war. The current direct cost for the war in Iraq exceeds $4,000 per household at 130 million households. This number could easily double once all the worn-out equipment is replaced, the troops are brought home, and the wounded are cared for. I often wonder how many die-hard supporters of the decision to invade Iraq would maintain their position if they had to write that check for $4,000? During World War II, everyone sacrificed. People worked eighty hours a week in the factories. Food and goods were rationed. People even recycled cooking grease to make ammunition. We were truly one tribe, and the all supported the all. With the current all-volunteer military, society essentially has people who wear uniforms to do all the sacrificing. The rest of us get to go to the movies.

Tribal thinking is in no way restricted to the uneducated. One of the most striking examples of tribal thought is embodied in the Bush Administration's policy of "the one percent doctrine." It states that if a potential enemy represents even a one percent chance of causing harm, then we have the right and obligation to attack first and eliminate the threat. This policy is about as tribal as it gets. It is a complete and formal rejection of proportional thinking. It is an attempt to justify the yes/no tribal reaction. If people behaved this way all the time, we'd all be dead. The proportional response relative to the amount of risk has been officially abandoned by the highest governmental power in the world and the people that dreamed it up have Ph.D.s.

The preceding discussion illustrates how tribalism affects thought. The logical, obvious contradiction of simultaneously demonizing the government and glorifying it is not obvious. In fact, most are oblivious to it. We want social order, but we don't want government-mandated social regulations. We want national security, but we don't want to pay for it. We say we support a war effort, but we don't do anything to support it. Government is the enemy, and yet government will keep us safe. Why do people keep contradicting themselves in this fashion?

We do this because of belief systems. Our perceptions of reality, our decision-making processes, are dominated by our beliefs, our ideologies. We can't raise taxes to pay for even what are perceived as essential military expenditures, because taxes are believed to restrict the market, and the market is king and must be revered, no matter what. We want personal responsibility instead of social regulations, but people don't behave in a responsible fashion. We say we are patriotic and totally support our military in the field, but make no personal sacrifice for them. I'm not arguing whether any of these policies are valid. I am arguing that they show how our beliefs control our thoughts. The belief generates an emotional response, not a rational one. This is a direct result of tribalism. People who are more tribal in nature are more prone to have these types of reactions.

How many times have we watched television interviews where the interviewee states that, "I want to vote for a person who shares my values." Probably about a billion times. But what does this statement mean?

What are values? Values are things we desire. Why

do we desire them? We desire them because they have properties that produce outcomes that we find to be highly emotionally significant. But how do we determine what makes outcomes highly emotionally significant? Our belief systems do. So, ultimately, our belief systems define what it is that people value. But belief systems also define tribal membership. So when a person says that they want to vote for "someone who shares my values," what they mean is that they want to vote for someone who is a member of their tribe. Being a member of the same tribe means the individual shares the same tribal beliefs. Generally speaking, what type of person is most likely to be a "values voter"? Those who claim to be values voters seem to align themselves with the political right. This is a further indication that conservative mindset is more tribal than the liberal mindset, as the values requirement is defined by the belief system. The more rigid and specific the values requirements are, then the more rigid and specific the belief system is, which is therefore less inclusive and more tribal.

Many books have been written recently that investigate why people from small-town America consistently vote for political candidates whose stated mission will be to implement policies that are against their own economic interests (Frank, 2004). Why are they inclined to vote for candidates who emphasize "winner take all" and trickle-down economics?

The answer is so obvious that apparently no one has apparently bothered to notice. They are *not* voting against their economic interests. They are voting *for* their belief system, their tribe. They turn on the TV, and they see what looks like the collapse of civilization. They see half of the babies bring born out of wedlock, drive-by shootings, gang violence, kids who can't read, drug abuse, 50% high school drop out rates, and the list goes on and on. The party of their choice claims that they will restore social order by re-establishing proper value systems as outlined in what they consider to be the most significant catalog of value systems of all, the Bible. The claim is that we should replace man's decadent secular laws with God's righteous laws. The party of their choice claims that they will eliminate the programs and the legal pollution that allegedly caused these problems. These criteria are extremely important to small-town America, and if the party of their choice creates a few hundred new billionaires in the process, then, so what? It doesn't matter to them. This is the basis of the so-called culture wars at the ballot box. It's the tribal response again, self-sacrifice for the good of the tribe, up to a point. So long as individuals can get enough to eat and their surviv-ability is not in question, they tend to remain loyal to the cause, even steadfastly loyal.

Continuing these arguments, why is humanism viewed by religious conservatives as such a dire threat to the na-tion? Humanism is the principle that people should be nice to each other and treat each other with respect and dignity simply because they are human beings. It defines a social order with no overarching enforcement structure headed by a deity. For thousands of years, religion has largely func-tioned as the final arbiter of moral authority. People should be nice to each other, because the religious codes dictate it and God demands it. Disobey the codes, and you will surely be punished, if not by man, then by God. If people follow the principles of humanism, then there is no need for the structure of organized religion to get people to behave. But religion identifies the tribe. Therefore, eliminating a primary need for religion is then viewed as a direct assault on the tribe. Without religion to hold the tribe together, it could fall apart. The animosity projected by religious conservatives towards humanism is caused by their view of it as a direct threat to the survival of their tribes. From their perspective, the two cannot coexist, and the rise of humanism necessarily means the destruction of piety, which will lead to societal collapse. This is the all-or-nothing, yes/no reaction again, which is a tribal response.

The specific beliefs followed are not important. Religious conservatives of all faiths react in a similar fashion. They all see social decadence and societal collapse as a product of the lack of an ordered society, and that following divine codes of behavior must provide that order. There has been a resurgence of religious fundamentalism all over the world, encompassing a wide variety of belief systems. They all produce the same tribal response. It's not the particular ideology that causes the tribal response. Cognitive dissonance will convince followers to accept as true whatever the belief system dictates. It's the emotional significance of the group ideology that is the controlling factor. The degree of tribalism controls the degree of emotional significance of the belief system, because the belief system defines tribe. The whole point of the tribe is to determine the "us." If belief systems define the "us," then belief systems are highly emotionally significant to the tribal mind.

There is another division between the religious conservative and the secular liberal that I would like to explore. Why is it that the secular liberals are such peaceniks and religious conservatives are much more prone to beat the drums of war?

Last Christmas, I watched the movie, *The Robe*, on PBS. The story was about the beginnings of the Jesus movement as portrayed in the Bible. The early Jesus followers were shown as being loving, open, accepting, tolerant, and forgiving against a backdrop of Roman oppression and brutality. I thought, *what a beautiful movement.* No wonder so many people joined it. But if I turn the TV on Sunday mornings, I sometimes see fire-breathing, shouting, condemning, intolerant conservative preachers who beat the drums of war (Hedges, 2006). They equate supporting military conflict with patriotism. Why do the followers of the Prince of Peace seem so anxious and ready to start shooting, while the godless secular liberals are running around with peace signs? Why does love of country equate with love of combat? Isn't it possible to love your country and abhor combat? I'm not in any way suggesting that war can always be wished away. The world is a very dangerous place full of very bad people who will do very bad things if they get the chance. The issue I raise is why combat is so desired. This contradiction between the principles of the Jesus movement and modern-day Christian conservative zeal for military action had always deeply puzzled me. It doesn't anymore.

The attitude of attack to defend is purely tribal. The reason these people appear to be so anxious to apply military force has nothing to do with religion. It is one of the most primal of all tribal motivations. Tribes came into existence for survival. The whole point of the tribe is to determine the "in" group and "out" group, whom to support and whom to kill. Combat is an essential component of tribal life, because primitive life was so brutal (Smith, 2007). If there is one activity that binds people together, it is combat (Hedges, 2002). It's as if the desire to experience this intense tribal binding is so great that some people actually act like they welcome war. It's the ultimate tribal cause, the ultimate quest. This is why many conservative preachers condemn the peaceniks as being unpatriotic, even though the peaceniks are putting into practice the teachings of Jesus Christ. When war breaks out, those that reject the conflict are viewed as unpatriotic, because they are rejecting the supreme source of tribal unity, which is war, and war is all about the survival of the tribe. To support war is then the ultimate projection of tribal loyalty. This tribal motivation is so strong that religious leaders often succumb to it even when it violates the very essence of their religious doctrines. Tribalism has such power over us that it can cause us to contradict some of our dearest and most sacred beliefs.

The preceding argument shows that tribal people are necessarily adherents of belief systems, such as religion, but religious people are not necessarily tribal. This is the valid logical condition of "A" causes "B," but "B" does not cause "A,"

As previously argued, belief systems define the tribe, and highly tribal people are then strong followers of belief systems, religious systems being the most prevalent. Other types of belief systems could be followed in place of, or in addition to, religious ones, such as political or economic ideologies. The criteria I have established require that some type of belief system be strongly followed or the person will not be regarded as highly tribal.

Adherence to belief systems is a marker and requirement for tribalism, but adherence to belief systems does not cause tribalism. To test this, we can look at the inverse condition. Do religious non-tribal people exist? If they do, we should be able to find religious liberals. Is there is such a condition as the religious liberal? Yes, they're all over the place. To deny the existence of the religious liberal is to maintain that only conservatives follow religion, and that is a preposterous claim. Religious liberals have faith, attend worship services, and truly believe in their religious doctrines. We don't notice them as much, because they don't make as much noise. I view them like Nixon's "silent majority." What kinds of characteristics do they present? They tend to act like secular liberals with the inclusion of deity worship. Most significantly, they tend to be peaceniks and don't equate the desire for reduced conflict as a lack of patriotism. It is possible to have faith in religious doctrines, love your country, and not have a bunker (tribal?) mentality that we are constantly under attack or need to be attacking. As Presidential candidate Mike Huckabee says, "I'm an evangelical; I'm just not mad at anyone." When I was in my mid-twenties, I had a very pious friend who taught me two lessons I never forgot. One was that religion is man's attempt to worship God. The second is that man's greatest sin is that man tries to be like God. I think some of these intolerant, condemning preachers need to talk to my friend.

The key point to prove, then, is whether the liberal mindset is less tribal than the conservative mindset.

We have established that intense tribalism uses belief systems to define tribal membership, which creates a greatly restricted concept of who is in the tribe. The condition of being less tribal would imply a more open means of tribal identification. The less restrictive tribal membership is, the more inclusive it is. Since rigidly following a belief system sets up strict requirements for tribal membership, less restrictive membership would necessarily require less rigid belief systems, which is exactly how the liberal mindset opens up the range of tribal membership. The definition of tribal membership is driven by the belief system that in the liberal sense is looser and more open. The Unitarian religion is a good example as contrasted against Orthodox

Judaism. The "us" then continues to expand as inclusion grows. Ultimately, as the "us" grows to include the entire human race, as with humanism, and the concept of the tribe is eliminated. There is no "us and them"; there is just "us," and there are no longer any tribes. Humanism when taken to its maximum extent then is the elimination of tribalism. The liberal mindset by definition is not just less tribal, it's ultimate extension is the elimination of the tribe.

The possibility of the elimination of tribes does not necessarily mandate the elimination of belief systems. In this scenario, people could practice different religions and still be considered as members of the same tribe. I believe this is the intent of the U.S. Constitution, but it doesn't seem to be working. It should then be possible to have a world where a wide variety of beliefs are followed, but we don't kill each other over it. This would be very, very difficult to accomplish, because it would require overriding our cultural and biological programming, and that will require a massive effort of education. The reason some people are tribal and some are not must be a combination of genetic and environmental factors. The option of eliminating genetic factors is not available for obvious reasons, but the environmental factors are. Realistically, this will take centuries, but it is possible to achieve.

There is an apparent contradiction in differing conservative philosophies that I must explore to validate my analyses further. Strictly following the tenants of a belief system is tribal, and religious conservatives are more tribal because of their belief in the strict adherence to a code of social regulations that are essentially Biblical in origin. This requirement restricts group membership and results in splitting the world into separate groups of followers and heretics. A fundamental goal of the religious conservative is to reduce human suffering and assist the poor. The economic conservative belief is that everyone must take care of themselves by harnessing market forces so as not to drag down the rest of us. They believe that regulations should be eliminated so there are no restrictions on winning, and if losers lose, that's their problem. One group wants to impose regulations on society, and another wants to eliminate them. How can they both be tribal if they want to do opposite things? These two groups are tribal not because of the policies they implement, but because these policies are implemented as a result of strictly adhering to a set of beliefs. One group defines themselves by rigidly adhering to a belief that it is best for society to eliminate economic regulations, and the other defines itself by rigidly adhering to a belief of imposing social regulations. Membership in either group requires accepting that group's respective belief systems, and individuals that do not are viewed as being outside of the group. Even though the two groups have contradictory belief systems, they are both tribal, because in each case group membership is defined by a set of beliefs. How can opposing ideologies be components of the same tribal genre? Why do they both tend to vote for the same political candidates if they have different goals for society?

The answer is abortion. This is the primary issue that ties them together. The Republican Party, as the reigning conservative group, has taken the position that it is completely opposed to abortion, which has caused the religious conservative group to join ranks with them, because they are so fervently opposed to it. It is and has been the lynch pin that holds them together, motivated by the extreme emotional significance that the position entails. This is an alliance of two separate tribes, not one tribe.

If a characteristic of tribalism is following the leader,

which is an application of strong centralized control, and conservatives are more tribal than liberals, then conservatives should be more supportive of strong centralized control. Is there any observational evidence of this?

Yes. Look at the way Democrats and Republicans choose their Presidential nominees. The Democrats use a proportional system that is chaotic, rough, and inefficient. This is exactly how democracy functions. It is very inefficient and requires a lot of infighting, and negotiating. The Republicans use a "winner take all" approach that is much quicker, more efficient, and inherently less democratic. Here the result is more important than the process. This reflects a desire for centralized control. Why? Because if the process is less democratic, then what is it? It has to be more centralized and authoritarian by default. Efficiency can only be obtained at the expense of democracy by using more centralized, authoritarian methods. The more authoritarian, the more tribal, because the tribe is organized under centralized control.

The political right is also a strong proponent of the Patriot Act. This is a law that gives the President the right to usurp constitutionally guaranteed freedoms if he deems that national security is involved, which is a huge concentration of power, hence much more authoritarian. The political left cries foul, claiming we only have the rule of law to protect our freedoms and that to ignore our system of checks and balances is a big step toward tyranny. The political right screams, "We don't care; just keep us safe." I am not attempting to justify either position. I'm establishing that the position on the right is more tribal because it relies on strong centralized control. Vice President Dick Cheney has often publicly stated that he wants to "restore" the power of the executive branch. I think "enhance" might be more accurate. Any concentration of power in fewer hands is by default more authoritarian and therefore more tribal.

There is even a legal ideology to support this movement, the unitary executive. It gives the President the authority to issue what are called "signing statements," where he can declare any law or part of any law unconstitutional and ignore it. President Bush has issued more signing statements than all previous Presidents before him combined. This is a tremendous concentration of power in the hands of one person and is therefore very tribal.

The one percent doctrine of attacking to defend is a concentration of power in the executive branch, as it is the executive branch that makes the decision to attack. The rationale behind it is tribal and so is its implementation as the decision is made by a central authority, and this is tribal.

The political right has become very tribal with its decision to eliminate possible threats with the one percent doctrine, suspension of the rule of law with the Patriot Act, concentration of power in the executive branch of government, and ignoring of our constitutional system of checks and balances with signing statements. All of these items reflect a move towards centralized, authoritarian control, which is a marker for tribalism. Whatever happened to the libertarian principles of Barry Goldwater? If he came back from the dead and saw what was happening, he would probably think he came back to the wrong planet.

One of the reasons the Republican Party has shifted so far to centralized control is the policies of the Bush Administration. In a tribal society, the leader sets the agenda, and the tribal warrior follows the dictates of the leader. Dissent is viewed as treason. I'm certain that there are many

Republican politicians who privately align themselves with more traditional conservative ideals, but remain mute (Bartlett, 2006). They cannot publicly take a stand against the leader. In the House of Representatives, the former Majority Leader Tom Delay had the nickname the "Hammer." He got that name for "hammering" Republicans. Do Democrats have party influence over the way their members vote in Congress? Yes, absolutely, but not to such an extent. There is much greater likelihood that members on the left side of the aisle will break ranks with party leadership, because the left is less tribal. The effective result of all of this is that our elected representatives don't represent the will of the people' they represent the will of the leadership of one of two political parties. The agenda of either party is set by whoever is at the top of the particular party, the tribal leader. This is tribalism in action.

A little tribalism is necessary for society in that it helps to establish social order. Chaos and "If it feels good, do it" isn't an effective way to run a country. The history of human social structure is very tribal, and democracy has only been widely employed for a few centuries. Perhaps we are still learning how to get along with each other within a democratic system. Before the emergence of the United States, most societies were ethnically and racially monolithic. The U.S. is a true melting pot, and maybe we haven't quite figured out how to make democracy work for everyone yet. Tribal influences are still here and are quite dominant. We still have a lot of work to do.

Tribal Structure of Taxation

Belief systems are very powerful motivators, and, as stated earlier, some people will lay down their lives for a belief. We need to investigate the conflict between self-sacrifice and self-interest to answer this question: does tribalism override the individual's self-interest, or does self-interest override the tribal interest?

Classic economic theory teaches us that people will do what is in their own self-interest. Is the self-interest of the individual realized by doing what is best for the group? Does the group's best interest supersede the individual's, or is it the other way around? Or does promoting the interest of either promote the interest of both? Perhaps this is a dynamic situation, and the answers depend on the structure of the group, how the individual is integrated into the group, and what the individual or the group is trying to accomplish. Let's see if we can shed some light on the subject.

This may come as a shock to some, but behavioral science has greatly expanded since Adam Smith wrote *The Wealth of Nations*. To make such a statement is tantamount to the highest level of blasphemy in capitalist America, but there are two problems with the "self-interest" economic theory. One is that human beings are rational, and the other is the meaning of "self-interest".

Adam Smith was wrong. People don't make decisions based upon their self-interest in just an economic sense. They make decisions based upon their perceived self-interest in an emotional sense. These perceptions are based in our belief systems, our culture. Economic decisions certainly are a subset of what falls under the category of self-interest, but they are not always the dominant motivation. Our belief systems define what our self interests are in primarily an emotional sense. Rational thought is an evolutionary advance on top of our core emotional nature. There is a great deal of ongoing investigation conducted by neuroscientists as to the nature, function, and integration of our rational and emotional characteristics. What is important to my arguments is not the ultimate elucidation of these phenomena, but establishing that both characteristics do indeed exist. I have enough experience in business and life to conclude that people truly are not rational. If people were rational, their decisions would be based upon what they need. They are not. They are based upon what people want. People have an insatiable desire for wanting things. To believe that people are rational and operate by "I need" is to dismiss the existence of the entire marketing and advertising industry. The whole basis of advertising is to convince people to buy things they really don't need. There is nothing morally wrong with wanting newer and better things. The economies of the world would collapse if everyone stopped buying new products. My point is that the human characteristic to be unsatisfied and always want newer things is essentially an emotional response, not a rational one. As I have mentioned before, it should be no surprise to anyone that people make very important decisions based on how they feel about an issue, not on what they know about the issue. I hear this from people all the time. When confronted with a problem, the initial response is usually phrased, "This is how I feel about it." The emotional reaction to the problem almost always supersedes the rational one, which is why most people can't succeed in business on their own. Business success requires making tough, rational decisions. Financial matters are no different from any other category of decision making.

Belief systems heavily influence what any individual desires and how they identify themselves. Some may join a convent. Some become soldiers and risk being killed. Some become martyrs. Some go to Wall Street and become brokers. Some have many children. Some physicians move to remote parts of the world, earn next to nothing, and heal the poorest people on the planet and some become cosmetic surgeons and make a fortune. Poor people give money to charity. Self-interest is not exclusive to economic matters. The self-interest component of Mr. Smith's theories is nowhere near universal and certainly not restricted to economic matters. Many decisions that people make are based on how they will be viewed by other tribe members. Status, prestige, and honor are huge motivating factors in decision making.

When I was a little boy, I remember that if a woman had a baby out of wedlock, it was looked upon as a terrible shame and disgrace. In today's world, half the babies are born out of wedlock, and it's no big deal. The motivation in the past to only have children inside the confines of marriage was generated by society, not a heightened sense of personal responsibility. The social pressures placed on the individual by the tribe, the tribal values, are the enforcement mechanism. So what happened to the enforcement mechanism? The lack of enforcement arises from the collapse of the community. People don't live in communities anymore; they live in buildings. We don't function as communities; we function as isolated individuals. For example, when I was very young, my parents bought us a swing set. There was no way my father could put that thing together. A couple of the other dads came over and helped us out. There was never any question that they would, and they were happy to do it. The assembly was like a barn-raising, and the yard was full of people. This is what I mean by community, a sense of duty and responsibility to help your neighbors.

Nowadays, many people live in houses with attached garages with no front porches and back yards lined with privacy fences in neighborhoods with no sidewalks. A service cuts the grass and shovels the snow. No one sees anyone. Houses have become cocoons of isolation. The community has died. Part of the popularity of portable MP3 players is that they allow us to carry our cocoon around with us and further maintain the isolation. Socialization has become an event that must be scheduled. It's a job, a task that must be compartmentalized and formalized. This is very unhealthy, as we are naturally an intensely social species. Is it any wonder so many are in analysis? Is it any wonder divorce rates are so high? Individuals need the support of the tribe, and, without it, we face enormous pressures on our own to make it through life. The issue of values and proper behavior is not just a family problem or a social problem, but an "everything problem." Our group environment heavily shapes our individual behavior and vice-versa. This brings us to the issue of how much energy individual gives to the tribe and how much is withheld. We call it taxation.

When people organize into groups, systems must be developed to determined who does what. How much energy does any one individual sacrifice for the group versus for themselves? These types of problems are worked out by the political economy, which establishes a balance between self-sacrifice for the good of the group and the self-interest of the individual.

There is a battle being waged here between how much private property the individual gives to the tribe, or state, and what the state does with it. Does the state keep it, or redistribute it, or trade it? This battle has been fought for millennia, and we are still fighting it.

Let us assume that the hunter-gatherer system was the initial framework of modern human society, and that framework allowed people to benefit from social cooperation.

Natural selection has added features to our minds, such as reciprocal altruism, that cause us to work together efficiently as a means of increasing reproductive fitness. The important operator here is "added." Evolution works as a series of cumulative changes. Organisms become more complicated as time goes on. This is true not only of physical structure, but also of behavior.

But these initial societies were egalitarian. There was no private property and no political power (Johnson and Earle, 2000). There was no need for systems that would distribute power and property. Even if we always were an "us" species, starting from the time humans broke away from the rest of the animal kingdom five million years ago, only very recently in our history, probably only the last ten of thousand years, did the distribution of private property and political power become a major issue.

Since organized societal behavior is a more complicated behavioral system, there had to be a time before it existed. Deeply rooted in our biological programming is the basis for supporting the "me" over the "us." This is a very strong motivation that we all carry in our minds today. Self-preservation is about as strong a motivation as there is.

So now we have the beginnings of a conflict of interest. These are the needs and wants of the individual versus the needs and wants of the group, or, in modern terms, the state. This conflict is and has been the subject of intense philosophical debate, and we have fought many revolutions over it.

Government is needed to provide a means to regulate and order large communities, which includes the distribution of resources. Since agriculture created leisure time, it allowed for the production of surplus goods. Surplus goods are what we today would call consumer goods.

These goods enhanced the quality of life. They are desirous by all and greatly increase survivability. Those that have the goods have the greatest chance to live, especially during shortages, as poor folks are the first to starve and freeze to death. The distribution of surplus goods has a direct bearing on survivability and for that reason is of the greatest emotional significance to the individual. That's why we keep having wars and revolutions over them. Our five million-year-old biology has only had to deal with these factors for about ten thousand years.

One of the primary functions of government is the collection of surplus resources for the state. It decides who gives what and how much. The method of collection of resources is taxation. Taxes then represent a personal sacrifice individuals make for the good of the tribe. But doesn't the tribal response cause people to be willing to sacrifice for the tribe? It does, but the willingness factor is directly proportional to how much is left for the individual.

Why are so many conservatives, including religious conservatives, so dead set against paying any taxes? The answer can be found in looking at the problem from a different angle. Conservatives, especially religious conservatives, can be very generous in making charitable contributions. When big disasters hit, these are some of the first people to open up their wallets and give. So what is the problem?

The answer lies in how the tribe is defined. Conservatives tend to look at America as being made up of many tribes that embrace many belief systems. A strong motivation against taxes, especially federal taxes, is that the money will go to members of other tribes that will be used to support competing belief systems. The last thing any true-blue tribal warrior wants to do is to sacrifice his hard-earned resources to a competing tribe. They want their money to support only their tribe, their belief system, hence the desire for private funding of organizations that render social assistance. Private funding provides the opportunity to see that the recipient is worthy of receiving the assistance and follows or at least is knowledgeable of the proper belief systems that will, in theory, elevate the individual to a point where assistance is not required. So if my analysis is correct, the campaign against taxes is still rooted in maintaining the viability of the tribe, not every tribe. This is why so many conservative religious leaders are so opposed to taxes.

No one wants to pay taxes, but the secular liberal or humanist mindset has a different definition of the boundaries of the tribe. They see the nation as one tribe, and the humanist views the entire planet as one tribe. It's the concept of, "We're all in this together." The more liberal mindset is less tribal. It does not use rigidly structured belief systems as a means of tribal identification, but a more open, inclusive, and loose structure. Isn't that what the Prince of Peace is trying to accomplish? Something about one kingdom on earth?

The liberal view has an easier time accepting the function of taxation as an unpleasant, but necessary requirement for the maintenance of the state. Civilization costs money. The Roman Empire wasn't built out of credit cards and home equity loans.

One argument I often hear about taxation from the right

is that the lower the tax rate, the greater business will be stimulated, and the greater the generation of federal revenues. Let's look at some numbers. Currently, US GDP is around thirteen trillion dollars and the federal budget is three trillion dollars. The government has just announced that the projected deficit for 2009 will be just under 500 billion dollars. That means that current federal taxes are 19% of GDP. Let's say 20% to be conservative. If we cut taxes in half to 10%, then that would generate an annual deficit of 1.8 trillion dollars. The economy would have to grow to thirty trillion dollars, or literally triple in size just to generate enough revenue to meet today's needs. If this massive deficit spending sparked a blistering annual growth rate of 10%, it would take twelve years to be able to finance today's needs of three trillion dollars. If we consider the hyperinflation that this level of deficit spending would create, the federal budget would probably be pushing up against ten trillion dollars by then with no increase in federal services from today's levels. In the meantime, the accumulated budget deficit would have increased another twenty or thirty trillion dollars.

You can't get there from here. The numbers just don't add up. There is a balance point between the level of taxation and maximizing economic growth while still meeting federal requirements. The argument to keep cutting taxes to stimulate growth only goes so far, and we probably have already gone beyond that point. I say this because federal deficits keep increasing. If the principle held true, then after eight years of big tax cuts, the federal coffers should be brimming with cash by now, but federal deficits keep increasing. If I may be so bold to offer a suggestion, perhaps spending has something to do with deficits. Perhaps if spending were cut along with taxes, then the principle would be more effective. If most spending can't be cut because of population demographics, the big potato here being Medicare and health care in general (Peterson, 2004), then tax levels have to be maintained. There's no escape from this hard reality.

Obviously, there are many other factors involved. Economic projections are essentially impossible to make. If it were known how to do it, then everyone could make a fortune in the stock market. My reason for making this illustration is that many people in the public sphere keep stating that we must continue to cut taxes. I'm not talking about politicians who spew that line out time and time again just to get elected. I'm talking about those who truly believe it. Why?

Our old friend tribalism is why. They just can't see the reality of the situation. The belief reigns supreme, and all of reality is filtered or altered to bolster the tenets of their belief system. The belief must prevail, and we can't let a little thing like reality get in the way.

Of course, there are many selfish, greedy people in the world, and those types would gladly join any organization that might be able to assist in increasing their personal wealth at the expense of the community. They want the benefits and pleasures awarded to them by living in this great nation, but don't want to pay for any of the societal machinery, the physical infrastructure, and the regulatory infrastructure that allowed them to earn that money. They don't realize or want to realize that without all of the systems that hold civilization together, such as transportation, water supply, courts, public education, law enforcement, communications, equity markets, banking, credit markets, federal reserve, customs, and so on, they probably never could have made any money in the first place, or someone else would have stolen it as soon as they made it. These are all highly regulated institutions that form the backbone of our civilization. The only tax rate these people really support is zero percent, which is the yes/no, all-or-nothing solution, which is a belief-driven response. They refuse to accept that there is a role in civilized society for a thing called a federal government and actually demonize it. They call their goal of zero taxation "starving the beast." They want to eliminate regulatory agencies by removing funding and forcing the federal government to shut them down. Let's explore the thinking behind this belief system of "starving the beast."

The conservative movement maintains that the individual is supreme and by removing economic restrictions the individual will prosper. Then society at large will prosper, because society is comprised of individuals. Unfortunately, many times some individuals will prosper at the expense of others. The gilded age of the late 19th century was a great example of this, and we are seeing it happening again as our nation moves in this direction today with the rise of the billionaire class while middle-class income has been stagnant for thirty years (Johnston, 2003). True, excessive regulation does inhibit growth. The more ways possible there are to make money, the more money can be made. But these folks aren't interested in reasonable regulation. They want zero regulation. The downside of eliminating all regulations is that it eliminates civilization as well.

The act of "prospering" necessarily requires social interaction. It is the manner that individuals interact with society at large that is critical. Cheating is not just violating any particular statute. Cheating in a behavioral sense means violating concepts of trust and fairness. Examples would be lying, stealing, defrauding, intentionally misleading, reneging on agreements, double-crossing, extorting, and any other repugnant behavior that people routinely engage in to make money. Let's look at how the world really works, instead of how some would like it to work.

In order to maintain civilized society, we have established the rule of law. People are required to behave in a certain manner so as not to harm or infringe on the liberties and rights of others. Social regulations are therefore necessary to maintain an ordered and stable society. This concept has been around for at least 3,000 years, because the Bible is filled with social regulations. If we did not have the rule of law and our institutions of government, the United States would function like Afghanistan and be ruled by brutal warlords and gangs. However, when it comes to economic activity, there seems to be a disconnect between understanding the need for social regulations and economic regulations. Let's look at this more closely. What are economic regulations? They are actually types of social regulations. All economic activity ultimately breaks down into interactions between individuals. They may appear to be interactions between people and "things," but there are people on the other end of transactions that are interacting with the same "things." Just because we use money, a universal medium of exchange, to buy things, people often lose sight of the fact that they still need other people to make the things they need to buy. All economic activity is then an interchange of decisions and behaviors between individual people. This is a type of social activity.

We have seen in the modern world what happens when societal regulations break down. Horrific carnage and brutality ensue. Genocide is all too common an occurrence. What happens when there are no economic regulations? Let's take a look at recent history.

In the 1920s, there was virtually no regulation of the equity markets. They operated like a gigantic pyramid scheme, and, man, did that pyramid crumble in the crash of 1929. So in the 1930s, the U.S. instituted the Securities and Exchange Commission coupled with an array of laws to regulate the equity markets. As of this writing, we have not had a downturn of anywhere near that magnitude since.

Then in the 1930s, the banks failed, which ushered in the Great Depression. The result was the enactment of regulations that dictated what commercial banks could and could not do, and the FDIC that guaranteed deposits up to $100,000. Banks still fail, but when they do, deposits are safe. These regulations restrict the profits banks can make, but that is an acceptable trade-off for stability. Frequent bank failures are catastrophic for our economy, as the 1930s taught us. The commercial banking industry has done very well over the last seventy years within the confines of a regulatory environment.

In the 1980s, the era of deregulation set in, which set Wall Street on fire. Equity prices exploded. Computer trading, financial derivatives, complicated schemes of leverage, and other trading schemes I can't pronounce let alone spell became commonplace. The first casualty of deregulation in the 1980s was the savings and loan industry. That was about 150 billion dollars in taxpayer bailouts in direct costs. Billions in profits were made by a few before the bottom fell out.

Then in the 1990s, clever (or corrupt) creative accounting practices were developed to circumvent accounting regulations, which were then used to defraud investors by falsifying corporate earnings. This contributed to, along with very loose monetary policy, the dot com stock bubble that burst and cost our economy literally trillions in wealth. The response was the implementation of the Sarbanes-Oxley regulations. These cost small companies a lot to comply with, but the nation had to do something to keep companies from cooking the books and defrauding investors or market liquidity would have dried up. This what is called "restoring confidence" in the markets.

Then in the first decade of this century, the geniuses of Wall Street figured out a way to bypass regulations for home loans by securitizing them and sold them all over the world. Brokers, dealers, middlemen, and CEOs made vast fortunes selling these bad loans and walked away with the commissions. Housing prices collapsed at a rate not seen since the Great Depression. Millions of homes went into foreclosure. The international credit markets seized up, and stock markets crashed all over the planet. The industrialized nations of the world had to mobilize to head off a collapse of the international banking system. It's probably going to take several years to unwind all the bad debt and untold trillions of dollars to restore the system. It doesn't get any worse than this. Why did the world's financial machinery fall apart in just a matter of weeks? The reason for the collapse was a complete loss of trust and confidence within our financial institutions. With all our fantastic technology and advanced culture, the simple emotional attribute of trust is what holds the world's financial systems together. The tribe cannot function without social regulations that instill trust, confidence and cooperation between members. Without these regulations and a means of enforcing them, the tribe will fall apart and that is exactly what happened to the international banking system. Maybe we should repeal a few more financial regulations so society can reap even more benefits of the power of the individual in the marketplace at the expense of the rest of us.

The irony of complete deregulation is that, when things do go bust, the taxpayer has to foot the bill. Most on the political right would call this socialism, which is the opposite of deregulation. This is because private investors won't throw their money into a bottomless pit. The few make a mess, and the many have to clean it up to keep from being dragged down into the mess. So we are supposed to release the power of the individual through deregulation to eliminate socialism and maximize growth, but it's OK to use socialism to fix the mess that excessive deregulation creates. Figure that one out!

Institutions hold complicated economic systems together. When these institutions are threatened with collapse, the result could be as catastrophic to the economy as was the Great Depression. We can't have a functioning economy without maintaining our institutions in a state of solvency, and we can't have institutions without regulations that define what they do. In other words, we can't have a stable economy without regulations.

How many debacles caused by deregulation does our society have to endure before people get the message that some regulation is necessary? All of these debacles were caused by inventing schemes of leverage backed up by leverage backed up by more leverage, until there was no hard capital backing up anything. I call this "selling nothing for something." Regulation is the only way to minimize fraud and the creation of invisible capital. Why? Simply, when money is involved, especially big money, people will do anything they can get away with. They cheat because they know they can. Without the constraints on behavior imposed by tribal laws, or social regulations, massive cheating is assured.

Civilization exists because of social regulations that maintain order and stability. It is the perceived lack of social regulations that has religious conservatives so upset and worried. They are afraid that the lack of necessary social regulations will cause society to collapse, and they are correct. The debate with them and the left concerns what is deemed as "necessary." In any event, there has to be some social regulation, or we can't have a functioning, civilized society. Economic activities require regulations for the very same reasons. Without necessary economic regulations, economic systems will collapse. We see this happening time and again, as I have just illustrated. Economic regulations are, in fact, social regulations.

Markets are amoral entities. Markets cannot enforce the principles of fairness and trust that are components of morality. What markets can do is correct for imbalances in the pricing of goods and services caused by supply relative to demand. Sometimes these imbalances are the result of just the market's functioning, sometimes they are the result of unfair advantages, such as monopolies, and sometimes they are the result of cheating. Only laws and regulations can correct for unfair advantages and cheating. If any particular market cannot be trusted, people won't use it or, worse, pull their money out of it. Liquidity will dry up, and that market could collapse, taking the entire economy down with it. Only laws and regulations can instill confidence in markets, just as rules instill confidence in sporting events, because without rules and regulations, the concept of "fairness" disappears as people will do anything to win or make money. As a result, confidence in that market or sporting event vanishes. History has shown time and again that when these processes are unregulated and spiral out of control, the inevitable correction causes intense economic carnage. This correction process is an economic analog of what happens to societies when social behaviors become unregulated due to the collapse of the rule of law. Carnage always results. When collapses occur, the carnage shows up in either dead bodies or bankruptcies, but it always shows up. Underneath the motivations that people have to be an "us," is the desire to support the "me." These are our more basic instincts. The "me" long predates the "us." Maybe this is what the ancient Biblical scribes were referring to when they wrote of "original sin."

If people evolved to engage in social cooperation as I allege, then why do we have so much trouble with cheaters? As others have written, this is due to anonymity. Originally, the prohibition against cheating evolved within bands of families small enough for everyone to know everyone else. If any one individual cheated, the whole group would know about it and punish or remove the cheater. This is precisely why violent crime is usually many times lower in small towns than in big cities. The size of big cities provides anonymity to the cheater or criminal. They can hide and get away with it.

Religious doctrines serve the same purpose. The major faiths of the Abrahamic tradition describe a God that is all-knowing and all-seeing. The reason these religious codes tell us that God sees everything is to eliminate anonymity. Violate the codes and face certain punishment, if not in this realm then in the afterlife. Religion then uses the same method of enforcement as small communities do. One must behave, because there is nowhere to hide.

Band structure itself was the enforcement mechanism that minimized cheating. Cheat and be punished or ostracized. As communities became larger and more complicated, anonymity became a factor, and traditional social enforcement lost its effectiveness against cheaters. Formal regulations would have then been necessary to provide an effective mechanism of enforcement. The larger and more complicated communities became, the greater the need for formal regulations in order to maintain stability.

No completely deregulated economic utopia is possible. Only the government, by force of law, can instill fairness and stability in economic markets. For example, in simple commercial transactions where the buyer and seller interact face-to-face, there is a great opportunity for the buyer to understand if he were cheated or swindled and by whom. In this case, markets can at least partially self-regulate, because the buyer will go somewhere else. I say "partially" because the buyer still has to figure out that he has been cheated and often times does not. The gold necklace may be fake. The mineral spring water may come out of a faucet.

Participating in large, complex financial markets further insulates buyers from sellers. There is no personal relationship with which to gauge the transaction. The size and complexity of modern financial markets provides anonymity for cheaters. The buyer not only doesn't realize he has been cheated, he also may not know who cheated him or how they did it. Even if the buyer does realize how he was cheated, it's too late. There is no recourse. These types of market activities can't self-regulate, because the cheater is getting the extremely profitable something for nothing. When the scam goes bust, the cheater just takes the money and walks away. The structure of the financial services industry greatly reinforces this behavior. Virtually all compensation is commission based. To make matters worse, the compensation of managers all the way up to the top is based on the profits generated by those underneath. This puts tremendous pressure on all to constantly improve profits. It's grow or die. There is no attitude of "good enough." The attitude is "make as much money as fast as you can anyway you can." Years ago, a retail stock broker told me that as long as the customer says "yes" then they are ethically justified for the manner the sale was made. That is, the customer is responsible for the decision, not the broker, regardless of what the broker said. When I was in my late twenties, I applied for a stock broker job. A leather tough manager took one look at me and told me that this wasn't for me. He said, "I cared too much about people." I actually once worked for a life insurance company that specialized in selling nursing home policies to the elderly. After receiving my script and training on how I was supposed to sell the product, I quit the very first day. This culture of "do whatever it takes to make the sale" has greatly contributed to our current financial crisis. The commission only, zero regulation culture breeds unethical behavior. Morality cannot thrive in this type of environment. Just as rules for social interaction are necessary for large, complicated communities, they are likewise necessary for large, complicated markets, because it is the size and complexity of markets which mandates the need for regulations to maintain stability and ethics. The only way to enforce behavior that instills trust in large complicated markets is through regulations.

So why do so many people remain convinced that economic utopia can only be achieved if we can eliminate all economic regulations? Because they are tribal people who diligently follow their belief systems. Their tribalism forces their decisions into a yes/no format, and a proportional response is not possible. The practical world answer to the regulation issue requires a compromise. Economic activity can and does thrive when a framework of reasonable regulations is installed for its operation. It always has.

Look at the tremendous economic growth the United States experienced between 1940 and 1980. But tribalism prohibits the fervent zero-regulation adherent from accepting this reality. No compromises are possible. Tribalism keeps the mind from accepting a proportional response where some regulations are acceptable. Instead, all regulations are viewed as unacceptable. The desire for zero economic regulation is no different from the extreme left's desire for zero social regulations and has the same effect on society: decadence resulting in economic or societal collapse. Not having any social regulations results in the elimination of morality, which is something that religious conservatives are fighting against. Again, I am no expert in religious beliefs, but why is it necessary for a person to live a moral life by following the social regulations of the Bible, but it is completely unnecessary for these very same people to follow these very same regulations regarding economic activities? Why is economic immorality justified? After all, economic activity is a subset of social activity. Why the disconnect? I never said belief systems had to make sense or be non-contradictory. This argument shows how powerful tribal belief systems are in shaping thought. They are so powerful that believers can contradict their own beliefs and not even realize it.

Another important way that the marketing of everything is having a negative impact on society is not directly economic, but academic. Some universities compete for enrollments by giving out more As. I have many customers who are university professors, and they all tell me the same thing. If they make coursework too difficult, enrollment falls, and their department's budget is cut. They say the students think that so long as they come to class and do the homework, they should all get As. If the professors don't give out lots of As, enrollment falls and budgets are cut. This is a huge problem with the marketing of higher education. Instead of maintaining rigid standards of excellence, scholarship is being turned into an economic commodity and marketed like toothpaste. Higher education is a great example of where the unrestrained free market does not provide the best outcomes. It is actually contributing to the "dumbing-down" of America, as scholarship truly has become an economic commodity. The American university system is in a race to the bottom to boost enrollments. Is it any wonder that Asian nations are becoming increasingly dominant in forging new technology and reaping the economic rewards that these developments bring?

Another question I have for those who believe that unrestricted markets always provide the best solutions for society is whether markets exist to serve society or whether society exists to serve markets. If markets exist to serve society, and they do, then why isn't it permissible to temper and regulate markets so they serve society more effectively? This is exactly the function the Federal Reserve performs when it raises and lowers interest rates and controls liquidity of the money supply. Why is it acceptable to have the Federal Reserve interfere and regulate the entire economy in order to control inflation and minimize recession, but unacceptable to interfere with specific markets by imposing regulations intended to instill trust, fairness, and stability? Economic regulatory infrastructure is just as necessary in maintaining a stable society as is criminal regulatory infrastructure. It is just as important for our tax dollars to be used for providing sufficient economic regulatory infrastructure as it is for criminal law enforcement infrastructure. "Starving the beast" is a very bad idea indeed.

Both taxation and federal expenditures are used as ways of implementing tribal political power. Both are essentially used to get people to vote for politicians of their respective tribes. If the federal government increases spending by 100 billion dollars and does not increase taxes at all, the net effect is to pump 100 billion dollars into the economy, which stimulates economic growth. Conservatives call this social welfare and vigorously oppose it, while liberals tend to support federal spending vigorously if it is intended to achieve a desired effect. If the federal government reduces taxes by 100 billion dollars and does not reduce expenditures at all, the net effect is to pump 100 billion dollars into the economy, which stimulates economic growth. Conservatives call this pro growth and vigorously support it, while liberals tend to oppose excessive tax cutting because it reduces much-needed federal revenue. This polarization comes from which segment of society benefits from the policy. As far as the net aggregate economy is concerned, these two examples are the same thing and produce the same outcome, which is 100 billion dollars of economic stimulation. So why are conservatives so adamantly opposed to increased federal spending, yet support any and all tax cuts while liberals do the opposite?

These conditions all reflect a tribal "us against them" position. There are several factors that delineate this tribalism. One is that if the stimulation is provided in the form of increased federal spending, the federal government can target the money to specific recipients. The opposition to this is based in the belief that those recipients may be members of other tribes. These types of programs are then labeled "social welfare" and are opposed by conservatives. If the money is spent on national defense, conservatives tend to support the expenditures, because the perceived safety of the nation ensures survival. An additional factor that must be considered when examining never-ending conservative support for ever-increasing government expenditures on defense is that these expenditures allow investors to "game" them in the stock market. When defense contractors get big contracts, their stock prices go up. About 90% of common stock is owned by less than 10% of the population. Stock ownership becomes more and more concentrated in the population as wealth rises. The top one percent owns a huge percentage of all common stock. This causes defense expenditures to function as a type of bribe that directly benefits wealthy political contributors, who in turn support the politicians who authorize the expenditures. Of course, there are many other types of federal expenditures that function in this manner (pork barrel spending), but expenditures for defense are easily the largest.

Another difference is the non-uniform effects of tax cuts across society. Since the tax cut is calculated as a proportion of income, the net effect is that most of the tax cut money is distributed to a small minority at the very top of the income ladder. If a working-class person gets a tax cut, the actual dollars received might be on the order of $500. If a super-rich person gets the same tax cut, the funds received might be on the order of $500,000. This results in a further concentration of economic and political power with the super-rich and reinforces the stratification of society on an economic basis. The belief supporting this policy is that empowering the upper crust is good for society, as this is where the leaders come from. Rich people, by virtue of their wealth, are thought to be better able to lead and direct society, because their wealth proves that they have special leadership abilities. This is a justification to maintain an aristocracy, actually a plutocracy. The tax cut enlists the support of the super-rich to finance political campaigns to elect politicians that will keep the tax cuts coming. This is all very tribal. The plutocracy takes steps to maintain its power in society. Tribes tend to do things that maintain themselves.

Tax cuts provide very little if any direct benefit to the working poor, because they hardly pay any taxes anyway. The extreme poor don't pay any taxes. Tax cuts can't help these people, because there is no tax obligation to cut. They can only benefit from direct assistance, which has to come from an expenditure. I'm not advocating expanding welfare, but giving someone a job that produces useful work that is financed by federal spending is a lot better for everyone than taking money for doing nothing, or even worse, incarceration. Many private sector companies have the federal government as their sole client. What's the difference?

The argument commonly made to justify the tax cut is that the working class will benefit from what are called "trickle-down economics." After nearly thirty years, there is no evidence that this happens at all. Since the late 1970s, the incomes of working-class people, particularly white male working-class people have been stagnant. No net benefit has been achieved (Johnston, 2003). As the owner of a successful small business, I can confidently say that I never experienced any trickling down from the rich. I experienced bubbling up from the bottom. I created a business out of next to nothing and grew it out of profits, just as countless millions of others have done. The point is that business formation is just like raising a child. It takes a lot of time, care, nurturing, and work. Businesses aren't created because a few rich guys got together and "did the deal." That's not a business, that's an arrangement. This is the difference between a wedding and a marriage. You can buy a wedding, but you have to work long and hard to have a successful marriage. Truth is that the vast majority of new jobs are caused by business start-ups, and many of those start with fewer than five employees and often just one. Ask these people how many wealthy investors capitalized their start-up. They most likely all used their own money or managed to get some kind of SBA loan. That's the way it works. Growth bubbles up from the bottom.

There is a common misconception that businesses are often formed from venture capitalists pooling money to finance start-ups, because they make interesting and prominently featured news stories. These types of companies are usually high tech firms that need tens of millions to get started, and most never go anywhere. Job creation comes from the many millions of small companies that never make the news broadcast unless they get robbed or burn down. When one million small businesses go from one employee to two, no one hears about it. When GM hires 500 people, it's front-page news.

Now, supply side conservatives would argue that my example shows that giving tax breaks to innovative risk-takers stimulates growth. I would tend to agree, but the big tax breaks have been targeted toward the super-rich who already have the money they can afford to lose in a speculative start-up. These people don't need to have their high-risk investments subsidized by the government. If they didn't have the money to throw away, they wouldn't take the chance. No one gave me a big tax break to start my business. There is some validity to the concept of supply side economics, but conservatives gave the tax breaks to the wrong sector of society: the super-rich.

Another technique that conservatives use to maintain the tribe of the plutocracy is levying much lower taxes on income derived from owning things, such as investments, instead of wages. As an example, billionaire Warren Buffet has recently announced that his federal tax rate was 17%. The combined tax load of federal payroll and income tax (which are two names for the same thing) for most of us is between 25 and 30%, if not higher. We are told that Mr. Buffet needs the lower tax rate so he will invest and not keep his money under a mattress. A tax is a prohibition of an activity. By taxing wages at a higher rate than investments, we are encouraging investments and discouraging wages. In fact, the return on investments is often enhanced by reducing the load of high tax wages on business. We see this happening all the time when jobs and production are moved offshore. It's not just the higher wages of the American worker that influence this migration, it's also the higher taxes on the wages.

If the free market is truly the final arbiter of the allocation of capital, then the government should not interfere with this process. If all income were taxed the same, this would remove government influence from economic decisions and capital would flow into whatever generated the most wealth instead of the lowest tax liability. This would be more inclusive and hence less tribal. I will never accept the argument that people need a special incentive to invest. People will always try to make money any way they can. Tax policy influences only how they try to make money. The issue is not that investments are inherently more beneficial to society than wages, but that, as the tax system is structured now, it is easier to make money with investments than wages. Thus, more of it is being made this way. The largest sector of GDP is finance at 20%, which is even bigger than health care. This means the most significant way of making money in America is moving money from one pile to another. Manufacturing is down to about 12% of GDP and continuing to contract (Phillips, 2006). These results can be directly linked to our tax structure.

Politicians keep pushing the concept of the "service sector" economy as a path to economic prosperity. That's just a lot of baloney. Nothing is more stimulating to the economy than manufacturing. A portion of every dollar that flows through my little company probably flows through at least several dozen others. When I look at all my suppliers and the suppliers to my suppliers, and so on, it is obvious how many benefit when I make a sale. China is not experiencing double-digit growth from a service sector economy. It is manufacturing that is propelling them forward. America cannot have the most powerful economy in the world if we all become massage therapists and interior designers.

Reducing the Tribal Effects of Taxation

I suggest that the first $10,000 of income from all sources be tax-free for everyone, no matter how much or little they make. This plan would incorporate no other deductions whatsoever. At the $10,000 threshold, every dollar past that would be taxed at a rate of 15%, the current payroll tax rate. My plan would eliminate all payroll taxes and lump everything together as one income tax. I would then linearly ramp up the rate to a maximum 25% at a higher income level of around $300,000 and then level it off. For example, at a $100,000 income the rate would be 18%, at $200,000 it would be 21%, and at $300,000 it would reach an ultimate level of 25%. No deductions, no exceptions, and all sources of income would be taxed at the same rate. The figures I have used are ballpark estimates chosen to illustrate how the system would work. They could be adjusted up or down as needed. The concept of having an initial large exclusion for all leading to a mild progression that levels off is what is important.

In conjunction, all profits that any corporation distrib-

utes to shareholders should be tax-exempt to the corporation. The tax on the distributed earnings would be paid by
the shareholder at their income tax rate, which eliminates
double taxation of corporate dividends. Corporations
would be taxed only on earnings that stayed inside the company and not distributed. This would provide an incentive
for corporations to distribute profits to shareholders and for
shareholders to buy and hold stock that had a good payout.

This plan is mildly progressive, which does not overly
penalize success. It allows everyone a $10,000 exemp-
tion that could be used for investment purposes or whatever they want. Instead of targeted tax credits, the initial
$10,000 exemption is universal and all-inclusive, which
is entirely non-tribal. The mild progressive nature of the
plan allows lower-income people to pay a lower tax rate on
investment income, which will help them to reach higher
income levels and accumulate assets. As income grows,
the tax rate increases on investments and all other income
up to the maximum.

The plan has several advantages. People who make
less than $10,000 dollars a year should not pay any taxes
at all. The initial exclusion would allow for a new class of
employment. Small businesses could hire a few part-time
employees and not be burdened with payroll or withhold-
ing taxes. I'm not advocating reducing the minimum wage,
but setting up a system where small business could provide
employment on an as-needed basis without any burden-
some tax regulations to deal with would be a tremendous
help and create many jobs. They wouldn't be career positions, but essential starting points. I am essentially suggesting the formation and legitimization of a tax-free wage
base for small businesses to help them get on their feet
and become established in the market place. This would

be a great way to offer a few hours a week of employment to stay-at-home moms, students, retirees, or anyone who has the time to make a few extra bucks. A thriving cottage industry can grow into strong businesses if given a chance to thrive. This is what I mean by bubble-up economics. So long as the employee is paid less than $10,000, no taxes are withheld. Simply issue a 1099-MISC to the employee at the end of the year. If employees have more than one job and exceed the $10,000 exclusion, it would be up to them to settle up with the IRS or the IRS to go after them. Full-time employees would still quality for the exclusion, but the employer would not have to withhold any tax until the exclusion limit was reached. Employers would only have to file the paperwork that they already do. In order for this system to work, it would be absolutely essential that the social safety net be paid for out of general revenues and not tied to employment, as there would be no more payroll taxes. Business should not be in the social safety net business. Government should take care of that need. America has to compete with the third world in the global economy, and this would help level the playing field and establish fragile new businesses here. It's a different world now, and we have to adjust to the realities of the situation.

State and local taxes should be structured the same way. Property tax, arguably the most regressive and brutal tax there is, would be eliminated and replaced with income tax. Taxing income makes sense, because at least there is income with which to pay the tax. Taxing property is brutal, because often property generates no income. If the property does generate income, why not just tax the income? This would be a tremendous boon to the accumulation of hard assets for everyone, rich and poor.

By treating all sources of income with the same weight,

this system is more inclusive and less tribal. The rate of taxation is determined by the amount of income, not the class of income. The mild progression gives relief to lower and middle-income people without pounding the top end. A huge benefit of this type of system is that it eliminates special interest tax credits with a uniform, no-exception tax policy that would essentially eliminate the influence of special interests in influencing taxation. My system includes elements of both the left and right and caters to no special interests, making it less tribal. It does utilize supply side economics, but targets entrepreneurs at the low end of the economic scale where most jobs are created, not the super-rich. Allocation of capital resources would be decided by what generates the greatest wealth, not the lowest tax liability. By taxing distributed corporate profits only at the shareholder level, the incentive to own equities is increased, and those investments can more easily provide income for people, all people.

The liberal view regarding taxes is that they are intended to support the needs of the people, not satisfy a belief. A great example is Social Security. Many conservatives act as though Social Security is the bane of society and has turned America into a welfare state. They think it must be privatized and removed from government control, but most people love it and want to maintain it in its present form. Those that wish to eliminate it are usually people that have more money than they know what to do with, or they are young, head-strong males that have yet to experience any of the hardships that life has in store for them. I felt the same way when I was twenty-five. After a few visits from Mr. Adversity, my appreciation for Social Security has grown tremendously. Those who want to keep it the most need it the most, and that is the vast majority of the population. Is Social Security a component of the welfare sate? Yes! So what? If that is what people want, then why not? It's supposed to be government of the people, by the people, and for the people, not the tribal belief of the market, by the market, and for the market. The liberal view in this case is less tribal, in that it is more inclusive as everyone can receive Social Security. The problems with financing Social Security are caused by changing population demographics. Initially, it was the many supporting the few; soon it will be the many supporting the many. Another problem with the financing of Social Security is that a growing percentage of income is being made from investments instead of wages, shrinking the taxable base that supports it. Adjustments will be necessary to maintain sustainability, but that does not mean that the whole program is defective or corrosive to society in principle. The advent of these "New Deal" and "Great Society" programs has created an independent elder class. Before the introduction of these programs, most of the elderly moved in with their children. If they didn't have children, they had a serious problem. People on the extreme right don't seem to realize that there is a cost associated with elder care with or without these programs. Perhaps we should eliminate social security and Medicare for one year and stop all payouts and taxation to illustrate this fact. It would be interesting to see how many will beg for the return of these welfare state programs after their parents move in, purchase horribly expensive private health insurance for them, and have to make personal sacrifices in administering elder care.

Another example of this type of tribal thinking is the resistance to government-funded health care. Currently, our health care -- or, should I say, our disease care system -- is a market-based system. There is a problem in this country with forty-seven million people with no health insurance, and I don't know how many tens of millions that are underinsured because they can't afford to buy the coverage they need. I'm not even considering the multitudes that are draining their life savings to pay for their health care.

Here are a couple of real-world examples of how an individual's life savings can be depleted. I have a friend who had a stroke a few years ago. He was self-employed and could no longer work. It took two and a half years to collect any Social Security disability. He had zero income for this period. If he had taken a menial part time job, such as pushing a broom for a few hours a week, he would have lost any possibility of getting disability. He was not yet sixty-two, so he couldn't get a reverse mortgage on his house. He had to sell his small house and move into an apartment. Because he was denied disability, he could not qualify for Medicare. His medical condition pushed his health insurance rates up to around $1,200 per month. So for two and a half years he had to pay the insurance and all living expenses out of the sale of his small home. To make matters worse, he had to get a lawyer to sue for his disability benefits and the lawyer took a third of them.

Here is another example. A few years ago, I talked to a barber who owns an old-fashioned shop in my area. He was about sixty at the time. He said he had a couple of operations, and his wife had a few medical problems. He ran a successful business and saved his whole life and had amassed over $300,000 in savings. Because of medical problems, his insurance rates were around $1,300 per month. The guy told me his savings had been depleted to around $130,000 and dropping to pay for medical bills and insurance. His retirement went from "comfortable" to "just getting by." A person can do everything right by saving and investing, and sickness can wipe them out right when they need the money the most. How many more people in

America have similar stories? There are statistics readily available for bankruptcies, but I would love to see the numbers showing how many people in their 50s and 60s had to consume the majority of their life savings for medical expenses.

How in the world can a market-based system be adjusted to provide services for tens of millions who can't afford for them? This is a contradiction in purpose. Market-based systems operate on the generation of profits, but it is not possible to generate profits by providing services for free. Businesses can't survive unless they can sell their goods and services at a profit, so they generally don't. There is no way to adjust this type of system to provide universal coverage without government participation to some degree. You just can't get there from here. There are probably millions of pundits, politicians, and people who absolutely refuse to accept this reality. Their tribalism causes them to follow their belief in markets so strongly that they become oblivious to these realities.

Components of a Tribal Belief System

Pulling all of my arguments together, it's clear there are five basic components to any type of modern tribal belief system. They represent an integration of all of the previous arguments including leadership, belief systems, non-verifiable results, and yes/no thinking. These components are essentially no different from the ones used by early leaders to project authority over their group. Perhaps we moderns are not as sophisticated as we think we are.

They are as follows:

Basic Principle:
A general statement of the belief

Operator or Force:
Some type of power or mechanism that drives the belief

Justification:
The evidence, whether it truly exists or not, that proves to the believer that the force functions as the belief predicts

Central Figure:
The individual or entity that originally created or transmits the belief to the world

Guidebook:
A written text or oral tradition that enumerates the tenants of the belief created by the central figure and/or the followers of the central figure

These components have always been present in any group-held or tribal belief system. They form a network of enforcement mechanisms that give the belief authority and dominance within the group. They are the end result of thousands of years of biological and cultural evolution, which has resulted in the manifestation of these five components as a universal component of the culture of tribal organization. The human mind responds to all belief systems in a similar fashion because of the action of these five components, and the response they create is the delineation of the "us" and "them." Let's examine scientific belief systems and compare them to religious beliefs.

Is it possible that the intellectual elite suffers from tribalism? Do people with an alphabet soup of credentials after their names fall victim to the same cognitive weaknesses as the rest of us? Absolutely! Tribalism is a universal human condition. The academic and scientific world is divided up and organized into groups, or tribes, by what are called "schools of thought." These are not physical demarcations, but divisions defined by theories or principles that actually function as belief systems. Academics often spend decades studying and investigating their respective fields. No one can put out that much effort for anything, unless they found the work to be highly emotionally significant. Scientific research often entails great personal sacrifice and time away from loved ones and recreational activities. Would you like to spend six months in Antarctica sampling ice cores in sub zero weather? Not me! This type of work requires tremendous dedication, or faith. One could make the case that the behavior of research scientists is no different from that of the religious zealot endeavoring to find some kind of spiritual enlightenment. The question then to ask is whether scientific ideologies function like a religion. If they do, and we react to them in the same way, then this would be an indication that our minds view them as the same type of stimulus, a condition we react to in a similar fashion.

A scientific ideology is based upon a belief. The belief would be some kind of theory or principle, such as evolution or the origin of human intelligence. Empirical evidence to support the belief may or may not exist. Even if evidence does exist, it may not be 100% reliable, because the gathering or interpretation of the evidence may be faulty. When empirical evidence is not available, rational arguments can be used to support the belief, such as this book, for instance. Sometimes arguments are employed to support a scientific belief that is based on false assumptions or bad logic. Empirical evidence and arguments, whether true or false, are all essentially the same thing. They are justifications for the belief.

The scientific belief is a definition that describes some natural process. The process is driven by some type of operator, a power or force that provides a means for the process to unfold. Examples would be gravity, or covalent bonding of atoms, or natural selection. This characteristic may be true or imagined, but in either case it is believed to be true. The actual operator, or force, is almost always invisible to us. All we can see are its effects. No one can see a jar filled with natural selection, but we can see a jar filled with creatures shaped by natural selection. This causes the actual force of nature to appear as an abstraction to our minds, because it exists outside our direct sensory perception. Gravity is such an abstraction, as are electric fields and potential energy. In fact, all properties of matter and energy are abstractions. These principles of nature are then ultimately constructs of our minds, even though they may truly exist in the world. They could even be considered as a type of myth.

We respond to religious beliefs in the same way. The thing that drives the outcomes of religious beliefs is always an abstraction. We never see the actual physical deity; we only see the outcomes that we believe the deity performs, and this constrains the deity to be a mental abstraction. Angels, devils, the Holy Ghost, the book of life, God, souls: all appear as abstractions to our minds, just as scientific beliefs do. So why do people more generally accept religious abstractions and often reject scientific abstractions? As previously argued, religious abstractions are an integral component of the evolution of our conscious minds. They are a part of us and are an essential component of self-identity which causes them to be extremely emotionally significant. For many, covalent bonding is not.

Kinetic energy is not. One could argue that these scientific beliefs are not emotionally significant, because most people have no understanding of them. This is true, but the lack of understanding often arises because they aren't emotionally significant, which causes them to be filtered out in the first place; as my personal example of my inability to learn chemistry illustrates. Modern scientific beliefs supported by empirical evidence have only been around for a few centuries while explanations of existence and being have existed since we had the cognitive ability to have them. Through the advance of technology, the scientific belief is an add-on to the base of the traditional religious belief. Our biology has preconditioned us to desire and accept mythical explanations of existence and being, but scientific beliefs are far too recent for any preconditioning to have occurred. An educational process is required before the scientific belief can be accepted. The two types of beliefs contain the same components, and both appear as abstractions and are treated by the mind in a similar fashion. They are essentially two varieties of the same thing and produce a similar tribal response such the "you people", "I'm right, and you're wrong," and the "us and them" reaction. Perhaps this is why there is such intense debate between the concept of intelligent design and evolution. As far as our mental processes are concerned, they are both two varieties of the same thing, like milk chocolate and dark chocolate. They both appear as abstractions to their respective followers and provide the same type of stimulus, which produces the same type of response. Intelligent design is more emotionally significant to its followers, and evolution is more emotionally significant to those who follow its principles. The rational nature of each of these principles is not important, because the justification for following them is viewed as rational by their respective followers; whether it truly is or is not. It is the emotional reaction to the principle that matters most, its significance to the individual that causes it to be followed.

Scientific beliefs do not originate on their own. There is always an originator, a creator of the belief. This person is often idolized as being something more than the rest of us. He or she is special, and is greatly admired, like a chief. The originator is an authority of the belief, and their teachings and writings form a guidebook for those who wish to follow the belief -- uh, I mean, the scientific principle.

Let's lay out a comparison between a scientific and a religious belief. I will use Christianity and evolution as examples, because most people can more easily relate to them. Any religion or scientific principle could be used.

Basic Principle:
Christianity: God sent Jesus Christ to earth for the salvation of humanity.
Evolution: An explanation for the existence of the tremendous diversity in the animal and plant kingdoms.

Operator or Force:
Christianity: God provides the salvation.
Evolution: Natural selection is the mechanism or force that causes the diversity of species.

These are both abstractions.

Justification:
Christianity: It's all around us. Anyone can plainly see the wonder and miracles of God's plan for us. It's in the joy of a baby's smile, the beauty of the mountains, the love we have for each other. Our existence is the proof.
Evolution: It's all around us. Anyone can plainly see

the wonder and beauty of the marvelous creatures that inhabit out world. Their existence is proof of natural selection.

The validity of either justification is based on the respective emotional significance to the individual. Cognitive dissonance and emotional filtering of information will reinforce the acceptance of the justification.

Central Figure:
Christianity: Jesus Christ came to earth to spread God's word. He is the messenger and as such is a very special person who should be admired, studied, and revered.
Evolution: Charles Darwin developed the theory of natural selection, which is a momentous event in human thought. He was a very special person who should be admired, studied, and revered.

This is "following the leader." Human social organization evolved to incorporate leadership roles.

Guidebook:
Christianity: The teachings of Jesus Christ are contained in the Holy Bible. All believers should study and honor it.
Evolution: Darwin wrote his teaching in *The Origin of Species.* It outlines and explains its principles.

A means of cultural transmission is necessary. Modern belief systems are too complicated to be transmitted through ritual alone.

I have listed five major components of a tribal belief sys tem. As shown, both religious and scientific belief systems contain these same five components. Think about it. It looks like we are dealing with the same animal. Comparing a religious belief system to a scientific belief system is like comparing a German Shepherd to a Siberian Husky. They are two varieties of the same basic thing.

This is starting to get interesting. If these two types of beliefs are treated by the mind in the same fashion, then people should react to them similarly. We have already discussed the tribal characteristics of religious grouping. What about scientists and scholars? Do they arrange themselves into tribes? They sure do.

They organize themselves into distinct groups that are defined by a belief, or schools of thought. Scientists are willing and even happy to undergo great personal sacrifice to validate and better understand the belief, just as monks do.

They fight wars with each other. Fortunately, the killing is omitted, but battles are fought with papers, studies, and arguments. These battles are often very heated, passionate exchanges. I've read books where one author goes after another by name. This is personal.

Arguments are usually polarized. "I'm right, and you're wrong." Just as with religion, the yes/no tribal response is common. If both are right, then funding and political power are divided between both "right" departments. It is to the advantage of one department if they are the only ones who are "right." This is the "us against them" in action.

They practice ritual events or holidays to celebrate the belief. We call them "seminars."

They have hierarchal management systems that oversee

and regulate the application of the belief. These are typically review boards and professional societies.

It is starting to look like scientific and academic communities behave just like tribes. Maybe that's because they are tribes.

Why would all these highly educated, rational, intelligent people behave just like any typical religious group that bases their beliefs on unverifiable ancient metaphysical principles? Tribalism is why.

Let's take this argument a step further and take a look at economic belief systems.

As previously stated, all of the major modern religions in the Abrahamic tradition are centered around a single individual. In the case of Jesus Christ, his followers believe that Jesus, a man, delivered a message to humanity and that message was the word of God. I have heard preachers use the term "the word" meaning that "the word" is the way to God. Believing in "the word" and the authenticity of its messenger is the path to salvation in the afterlife and will bring happiness and tranquility in this life. In fact, salvation can only be achieved by believing in the message. The deliverance of the message ushered in a new era on earth. A new kingdom had begun. Here we have a man, a message, and a belief. Following the dictates of the message will achieve the desired result of a happy, fulfilled life and salvation in the afterlife. This is essentially a new prosperity, a new age. The message also tells us that God is an all-powerful force in the universe that provides the means for these predictions to come true.

Ronald Reagan was a pious man who believed deeply

in God. Ronald Reagan had a message to deliver. The message was that there is an all-powerful force in the world that can solve all problems. He who believes in the force and follows its dictates will be assured prosperity. This force is a divine gift bestowed upon us as Americans through our democratic system of government. This force is the marketplace. The only way to achieve true prosperity is to implement the marketplace to its maximum capability, and that requires a zero-regulation economy, which will usher in a new era, a new age. This implementation is the essence of America, and to reject it in the slightest or alter it is taken as being unpatriotic or even treasonous. His followers believe that the free market economy is a necessary component of freedom, which is essentially a divine right. Rejection of the zero regulation economy can even be looked upon as a type of blasphemy.

Ronald Reagan was the central leadership figure required for this belief system. Jesus Christ served this very same purpose. The people would not have accepted the word of God if it were a voice from the sky. It had to come from the mouth of a man, a tribal leader.

These two examples are mirrors of each other. In both cases, we have a man delivering a message, and all-powerful force that enables the message to be implemented. It is believed that following the dictates of the message will achieve the desired outcome and the all-powerful force will provide the means of implementing the desired outcome. These are the components of a tribal belief system.

Does the Reagan belief system have the same five core components that scientific and religious beliefs have? Let's list them.

Basic Principle:
Economic prosperity can only be obtained in a zero
regulatory environment. Government is a hindrance to
prosperity and should be minimized from people's lives.

Operator or Force:
The free, unrestricted capitalistic market will provide the
means of achieving prosperity. Again, this is an
abstraction, as we can only directly observe the effects
of capitalism.

Justification:
It's all around us. All of the prosperity that exists was
created by capitalism, so the fewer restrictions and
regulations, the more prosperity capitalism will create.
The emotional significance of the justification reinforces
its validity.

Central Figure:
Ronald Reagan was the charismatic voice that delivered
the word of the unrestrained free market. The idea had
long existed, but Reagan spoke the words that enacted
the policy. In a fashion similar to Jesus Christ, Reagan
was the deliverer of the message. Because he was the
deliverer, he is a special person and should be revered.
During the current (2008) Republican Presidential
campaign, it was obvious that Reagan's name was
evoked more times than any other figure. His followers have essentially deified him. For example, I have
had many people tell me that all of the growth the
economy has experienced during the last nearly thirty
years is directly the result of Ronald Reagan. To believe
this is to believe that without the Reagan Presidency,
since 1980, no one would have tried to make any money.
It also does not explain how the economy ever grew

before his tenure. This is what I mean by deification. Before Reagan, nothing mattered. After Reagan, everything mattered. The new age had begun.

The leadership requirement is fulfilled.

Guidebook:
Adam Smith wrote *The Wealth of Nations*, which attempts to prove that people will naturally always act in their own self-interest, so society should allow everyone to do just that, maximizing prosperity. Thus, society as a whole will benefit.

All five components are present.

Do the followers of Reagan act like a tribe? Sure do. They call themselves free market conservatives or supply side conservatives. They claim that liberals are followers of Keynesian economics as if this were some kind of un-American activity by members of a different tribe. Never mind that Keynesian principles had been employed for fifty years with great success. This was before the dawn of the new age, so his principles are blamed for a host of problems that the new age had supposedly overcome, because tribalism causes the followers of supply side economics to believe that government participation in economic matters always makes things worse. Perhaps if they had lived through the Great Depression they might have a different viewpoint. But then again, perhaps not. The belief always wins out.

What about other political belief systems, such as democracy, communism, socialism, fascism, and any other "ism" you can think of" Not to belabor the point, but they all have originator figures: Hitler, Mao, Lenin, Trotsky,

Madison, and the like. They all have guidebooks, often written by the originator. They all have an overarching principle powered by some abstract force created by a type of social organization. And they all tout the wonderful benefits of their belief system, no matter how badly screwed up everything is. They believe it is so, so it is so.

My arguments provide what I hope is a very convincing rationale that religious, scientific, political, and economic belief systems are arranged and function in the same manner. Our minds should then respond to this similar stimulus in a similar fashion, that of tribalism. The belief system defines the tribe, and all belief systems function this way. This characteristic of the mind is an innate tendency installed in humans by natural selection to improve reproductive fitness by organizing us into groups. All of examples of the five components of a tribal belief system include an originator, which is essentially "following the leader." The teachings of the revered and admired have greater weight and persuasive effect than just anyone's words. We turn to our leaders for guidance and safety. This attitude that we all share gives credibility to belief originators. The same innate tendencies that cause people to follow the leader cause them to follow the teacher of the belief. One way leaders lead tribes is to teach the tribe what to believe. The emotional significance of the communal belief unites the tribe behind the leader. The belief defines the tribe.

These five criteria are essential elements of successful, widespread, tribal belief systems. The mind responds to all belief systems that possess these criteria in the same tribal fashion, whether it is God, the marketplace, ghosts, communism, karma, or any other ideology. The particular belief or type of belief does not matter. It's all the same. It's tribalism. It's us against them.

Concluding Remarks

The arguments I have presented indicate that the primary division between the religious conservative and secular
liberal is not based upon differing ideology. The difference
is based in strong tribalism, versus little or no tribalism.
This was not my intention when I started this project. I
originally wanted to investigate modes of thinking and how
ideology influences the way we think. As my arguments
developed, I have concluded that it's not the ideology that
alters the way we think; it's tribalism. The actual ideology
is relatively unimportant. It is the intensity of the tribal response that causes individuals to adhere to a belief system,
no matter what that belief system or ideology is. The belief
system defines to the individual what is and is not emotionally significant, because the belief system identifies the "in
group," the "us," and the "us" is a necessary component of
survival with its heightened emotional significance. The
concept of self-identity is directly tied to the "us." These
beliefs define reality and provide a foundation of conscious
existence itself. What we believe is in essence what we are,
and beliefs are a fundamental component of both the evolution of society and the conscious mind. These beliefs are
essentially sacred to the individual, giving them the highest
emotional significance. The degree of emotional significance activates how strongly cognitive dissonance reshapes
our perceptions of reality. The intensity of the reaction of
dissonance is set by the degree of tribalism, because the
more tribal the individual, the greater the emotional significance of the belief system and the greater reality is altered
by dissonance. Tribal people will follow whatever belief
system is culturally transmitted to them so long as they per-
ceive it as emotionally significant and communally shared.
Ultimately this perception is the result of genetic and environmental factors. The devout Muslim, the orthodox Jew,

and the evangelical Christian all have minds that react in a similar fashion. Any one could be transplanted at birth and become the other if exposed to the same cultural influences.

It is the degree or intensity of affiliation to the belief system that alters our thinking, not the actual belief system itself. The belief system is the foundation of tribal identity. A tribal person is one who strongly adheres to the doctrines and rituals of belief systems regardless of the what the belief system is. Human thought is greatly altered by the embrace of any belief system. Tribal people are strong adherents to the doctrines of belief systems and non-tribal people are much less affected. This is what I have concluded.

BIBLIOGRAPHY

Atran, Scott. 2002. *In Gods We Trust, the Evolutionary Landscape of Religion*. New York: Oxford University Press.

Barrett, Louise, and Robin Dunbar, and John Lycett. 2002. *Human Evolutionary Psychology*. Princeton, N.J.: Princeton University Press.

Bartlett, Bruce. 2006. *Impostor, How George W. Bush Bankrupted America and Betrayed the Reagan Legacy*. New York: Doubleday.

Behar et al., *The Dawn of Human Matrilineal Diversity, The American Journal of Human Genetics*. (2008) doi: 10.1016/ ajhg.2008.04.002

Boyer, Pascal. 2001. *Religion Explained, The Evolutionary Origins of Religious Thought*. New York: Basic Books.

Carter, Rita. 1998. *Mapping the Mind*. Los Angeles: University of California Press.

Churchland, Patricia Smith. *Studies in Neurophilosophy*. Cambridge. MA.: MIT Press.

Clark, William and Grunstein, Michael. 2000. *Are We Hardwired? The Role of Genes in Human Behavior*. New York: Oxford University Press.

Dawkins, Richard. 2006. *The God Delusion*. New York: Houghton Mifflin.
Dennett, Daniel. 2006. *Breaking the Spell, Religion as a Natural Phenomenon*. New York: Viking.

De Wall, Frans. 2005. *Our Inner Ape*. New York: Riverhead Books.

Frank, Thomas. 2004. *What's the Matter with Kansas?* How Conservatives Won the Heart of America. New York: Metropolitan Books.

Gardner, Howard. 2004. *Frames of Mind, The Theory of Multiple Intelligences*. New York: Basic Books.

Goldberg, Elkhonon. 2001. *The Executive Brain, Frontal Lobes and the Civilized Mind*. New York: Oxford University Press.

Goldberg, Elhonon, 2005. *The Wisdom Paradox*. New York: Gotham Books.

Greenspan, Stanley, and Shanker, Stuart. 2004. *The First Idea, How Symbols, Language, and Intelligence Evolved From Our Primate Ancestors to Modern Humans*. Cambridge, MA: Da Capo Press.

Hammer, Dean. 2004. *The God Gene, How Faith is Hardwired Into Our Genes*. New York: Anchor Books.

Harris, Sam. 2004. *The End of Faith, Religion, Terror and the Future of Reason*. New York: W. W. Norton & Co.

Hauser, Marc. 2006. *Moral Minds, How Nature Designed Our Universal Sense of Right and Wrong*. New York: Harper Collins Books.

Hedges, Chris. 2002. *War is a Force That Gives Us Meaning*. New York: PublicAffairs Books.

Hedges, Chris. 2006. *American Fascists, The Christian Right and the War on America*. New York: Free Press.

Johnson, Allan and Earle, Timothy. 2000. *The Evolution of Human Societies*. Stanford, CA.: Stanford University Press.

Johnston, David K. 2003. *Perfectly Legal*. New York: Penguin Group.

Joyce, Richard. 2006. *The Evolution of Morality*. Cambridge, MA: MIT Press.

O'Shaughnessy, Nicholas Jackson. 2004. *Politics and Propaganda, Weapons of Mass Seduction*. Ann Arbor, MI: The University of Michigan Press.

Peterson, Peter G. 2004. *Running on Empty*. New York: Farrar, Straus and Giroux.

Phillips, Kevin. 2006. *American Theocracy*. New York: Viking.

Pinker, Steven. 1997. *How the Mind Works*. New York: W. W. Norton and Co.

Pinker, Steven. 2002. *The Blank Slate, The Modern Denial of Human Nature*. New York: Viking.

Richards, Julia E. and Hawley, R. Scott. 2005. *The Human Genome*. Burlington, MA.: Elsevier Academic Press.

Ridley, Matt. 1996. *The Origins of Virtue, Human Instincts and the Evolution of Cooperation*. New York: The Penguin Group.

Ridley, Matt. 2003. *Nature via Nurture*. New York: HarperCollins Publishers.

Sanderson, Stephan K. 2001. *The Evolution of Human Sociality, A Darwinian Conflict Perspective*. Lanham, MD.: Rowman & Littlefield Publishers.

Smith, David Livingstone. 2007. *The Most Dangerous Animal, Human Nature and the Origins of War*. New York: St. Martin's Press.

Tancredi, Laurence. 2005. *Hardwired Behavior, What Neuroscience Reveals abut Morality*. Cambridge, MD.: Cambridge University Press.

Tattersall, Ian. 1998. *Becoming Human, Evolution and Human Uniqueness*. Orlando, FL: Harcourt Brace & Co.

Tavris, Carol and Aronson, Elliot. 2007. *Mistakes Were Made (but not by me)*. Orlando, FL: Harcourt, Inc.

Wade, Nicholas. 2006. *Before the Dawn, Recovering the Lost History of Our Ancestors*. New York: The Penguin Press.

Proof

Made in the USA